Begging as a Path to Progress

Begging as a Path to Progress

Indigenous Women and Children and the Struggle for Ecuador's Urban Spaces

KATE SWANSON

The University of Georgia Press • Athens and London

Parts of chapters 1 and 5 were previously published in
Antipode, 2007, vol. 39: 708–28. © Blackwell Publishing. Used
by permission of the publisher. A shorter version of chapter 4
was previously published in *Gender, Place, and Culture* 14 (6):
703–20. © 2007 by Routledge, part of the Taylor and Francis
Group. Used by permission. http://www.tandf.co.uk.

Printed digitally in the United States of America

Library of Congress Cataloging-in-Publication Data

Swanson, Kate, 1973–
    Begging as a path to progress : indigenous women and
children and the struggle for Ecuador's urban spaces / Kate
Swanson.
        p. cm. — (Geographies of justice and social
transformation)
    Includes bibliographical references and index.
    ISBN-13: 978-0-8203-3180-5 (hardcover : alk. paper)
    ISBN-10: 0-8203-3180-5 (hardcover : alk. paper)
    ISBN-13: 978-0-8203-3465-3 (pbk. : alk. paper)
    ISBN-10: 0-8203-3465-0 (pbk. : alk. paper)
    1. Indians of South America—Urban residence—Ecuador—
Quito. 2. Indian women—Ecuador—Quito—Economic
conditions. 3. Indian women—Ecuador—Quito—Social
conditions. 4. Indian children—Ecuador—Quito—Economic
conditions. 5. Rural-urban migration—Ecuador—Quito.
6. Quito (Ecuador)—Social conditions. 7. Quito (Ecuador)—
Economic conditions. I. Title.
    F3721.1.Q55S93 2010
    307.2'41608998086613—dc22   2009030039

British Library Cataloging-in-Publication Data available

To Sandy Luzmila

CONTENTS

ILLUSTRATIONS

ACKNOWLEDGMENTS

A twelve-year-old indigenous girl inspired the research for this book. During my first visit to Ecuador in March 2002, I encountered her often while exploring Quito's main tourist districts. This girl was clever, and she quickly deduced that my husband was an easy mark. Whenever we approached, she would grab the nearest child, rush across the street, and extend her hand while making pleading gestures. It worked every time, and she frequently walked away with a slight grin on her face. This girl, whom I later came to know, intrigued me; I wanted to learn more about her life. Not surprisingly, my initial assumptions about her were wrong. Like many, I believed that she was homeless and slept on the streets. Because I never saw any adult males with her, I wrongly believed that she and her siblings had been abandoned by their father. This image of the poor, single-parent, female-headed family fit into the preconceived notions I had developed surrounding Latin American street children. Then I began asking questions. As noted by Doolittle (2001), there is a big difference between looking and seeing.

There were many people who helped me learn how to "see," likely too many to acknowledge here. While I have done my best to be thorough, I suspect it is inevitable that I have overlooked someone in my efforts to offer thanks to all. Please accept my apologies for all those I may miss. Know that I deeply appreciate the support, encouragement, and assistance that I have received over the last several years.

To begin, I would like to extend my heartfelt thanks to the community members of Calhuasí for graciously sharing their lives and stories with me. These stories have moved me in so many ways, and I hope this book helps motivate people to challenge some of the injustices Calhuaseños endure. Mercedes, Antonio, Elsa, Maribel, Victor, and Miriam taught me so much about life in the community. Agustín and Manuela were especially helpful and I thank them, along with Silvia, Beatriz, Marcia, Cenaida, Sandy, and Jefferson, for welcoming me into their family. Much appreciation also goes to Segundo Manuel Poaquiza Poalasin and to José Antonio Pombosa Lasluiza for supporting my research in their village.

Janeth Gavilanez from the Fundación Don Bosco was a key facilitator for this research. I thank her for the tremendous assistance she gave me, but most of all for her friendship. The staff and volunteers at the Fundación Don Bosco were very kind and helpful throughout my field research. Padre Pio Baschirotto, Patricia Wattel, Susana Proaño, Rosa Chiza, Ximena Castillo, Francisco Carrión, Enrico Ferrati, Rosa Arias, and Simón Zimmer merit special mention.

José Maldonado Córdova was also instrumental in furthering my understanding of Quichua culture and language. I thank him for being both my teacher and my friend.

Of course, I owe tremendous thanks to both Sue Ruddick and Amrita Daniere at the University of Toronto for guiding me through this project, which began as a PhD dissertation. I feel honored to have worked with both of these exceptional women. Katharine Rankin and Gunter Gad often offered thought-provoking comments, for which I am deeply appreciative. Joe Hermer deserves many thanks for sharing his brilliant insights over coffee. I am very happy to have had Maureen Hays-Mitchell and Minelle Mahtani involved in the final stages of my dissertation, both of whom pushed me to develop key ideas. Virginia Maclaren also merits particular gratitude for supporting my decision to move my focus beyond Asia and into Latin America in the first place.

My friends at the University of Toronto and beyond provided much intellectual stimulation and after-hours diversion. Some of these individuals include Deborah Cowen, Stephanie Hart, Zoë Meletis, Sharlene Mollett, Yogendra Shakya, Tom Slater, Luisa Veronis, Alan Walks, and Anne Wu. Alana Boland and Scott Prudham provided direction and support during the early stages of my dissertation work. Grant Hudolin deserves special mention for his tremendous assistance with maps. I also owe many thanks to John Vigna, Elisabeth de Mariaffi, and Jennifer Kohm for advice on how to get my fingers moving on the keyboard. Jennifer merits particular gratitude for always providing me with a place to call home when I was in Toronto.

My fellow Ecuatorianistas must be thanked for their friendship, support, and insight into all things Ecuadorian (and more). These include Marc Becker, Chad Black, Ernesto Capello, Joe Eisenberg, Chris Garcés, Esben Leifsen, Kenny Kincaid, Chris Krupa, Elizabeth Roberts, Brian Selmeski, and Emily Walmsley. I am deeply indebted to Marc Becker, in particular, for always answering my many questions and for providing such wonderful feedback on my work. At FLACSO-Ecuador, I would like to thank Adrián Bonilla, Carlos de la Torre, Fernando García, Gioconda Herrera, Marcia Maluf, Carmen Martínez, Alicia Torres, and Alison Vásconez. Thanks also go to Liisa North for first networking me with FLACSO.

I was very fortunate to receive much financial assistance throughout the length of this research project. I gratefully acknowledge support from the International Development Research Council of Canada, the Social Sciences and Humanities Research Council of Canada, the Ontario Graduate Scholarship, the Sir Val Duncan Travel Award, the Frank M. Waddell Scholarship, the Connaught Scholarship, the John Robertson Bequest at the University of Glasgow, and the Department of Geography at the University of Toronto.

After finishing my degree at the University of Toronto, I spent two and a half years as a postdoctoral research fellow at the University of Glasgow in Scotland. This gave me a wonderful opportunity to really work through some of the ideas in this book. At the University of Glasgow, I'd like to thank John Briggs, Sophie Bond, Andy Cumbers, Simon Drew, Gesa Helms, Leah Gibbs, John Jansen, Jennifer Lea, Hayden Lorimer, Stella Lowder, Geraldine McDonald, Kim McKee, Jo Norcup, Ulrich Oslender, Ronan Paddison, Geraldine Perriam, Chris Philo, Paul Routledge, Jo Sharp, Rhian Thomas, and Susan Waldron—all of whom either contributed to my work or helped me maintain my sanity during Glasgow's dark, dreary winters. A special word of thanks goes to Chris Philo for being such an inspirational mentor and an all-around wonderful human being. Additional thanks to Leah Gibbs and Jo Norcup for being fabulous. Mike Shand and Olive Pearson graciously helped me with all things cartographic. During my time in Britain, I also benefited from the advice of numerous brilliant scholars, too many to name here. However, I would like to send out a special word of thanks to Noel Castree and Deborah Dixon, both of whom skillfully guided me through my early forays into the world of publication. Whether he knows it or not, Erik Swyngedouw also helped shape this work for the better by asking me a series of challenging questions at a talk at the University of Manchester.

The final stages of this book took place at San Diego State University. Here, I'd like to thank all of my new colleagues for giving me the time, space, and support to finish this manuscript, which was certainly challenging as a new faculty member—additionally so because I showed up for my new job six-months pregnant. Throughout this, Stuart Aitken, the departmental chair, has been so supportive and welcoming that I cannot thank him enough. I'd also like to extend my gratitude to Samuel Cortez and Denise Goerisch for helping me get the manuscript into final submission shape.

At the University of Georgia Press everyone has been a delight to work with. Foremost, I'd like to thank Nik Heynen for inviting me to submit this manuscript to the Geographies of Justice and Social Transformation series. I'm very happy to be a part of it. Nik is an inspirational scholar who does fabulous work, and I hope I can follow in his footsteps. Many thanks also to Andrew Herod and Melissa Wright for coediting the series. Derek Kristoff has been an excellent editor; I thank him for his advice and patience and for his timely yet gentle nudging as deadlines approached. Susan Silver has been a wonderful and meticulous copyeditor; this book is better because of her. As a reviewer, Craig Jeffrey provided superb feedback. Thanks also to Jon Davies and John McLeod and to everyone else behind the scenes for helping with the production of this book.

My parents, Keith and Nancy Swanson, have been so supportive throughout the length of this project, even though I suspect they wish I had chosen a project closer to home. Both have read almost everything I have written on this subject and have provided excellent critical feedback. My big brother, Andrew Swanson, and my sister-in-law, Tiffany Islip, provided much advice on how to navigate the world of academia. They, along with my niece Gabriella, also provided a loving home for the Ecuadorian street dog we brought back to North America. My in-laws, Bev, Tim, Megan, and Peyton Jones have also been very supportive and understanding, especially since I always seem to be out of the country during family functions. My grandparents, John and Mary Van Nest and Wilfred and Margery Swanson, have always encouraged me and expressed genuine interest in my work, for which I am very grateful. Unfortunately, three of my grandparents passed away during this project and I miss them dearly. Only my grandma Mary Van Nest survives; at ninety-four years of age, she remains a great inspiration to me.

Finally, I would like to thank my most immediate family. My dog, Kiva, traveled to Ecuador with me and ended up becoming a fantastic research assistant; I could not have found a better one. Her companionship has been a tremendous comfort throughout the last decade. I'd like to thank my son, Dimitri, for providing a compelling incentive to get my manuscript finished. It was a tight deadline but I somehow managed to finish it a few weeks before his birth. Since then, I cannot exactly thank him for helping me complete this project, but I can thank him for helping me work on my time management skills. Lastly, I wish to express my deepest gratitude to my best friend and husband, Greg Jones. Greg has lived with me through this project since its beginnings and knows its intricacies better than anyone. His keenly critical mind constantly challenges me to rethink and refine my arguments—something that has only made this work stronger. I cannot thank Greg enough for his tremendous support.

Begging as a Path to Progress

Introduction

Unraveling Myths

A young indigenous girl approximately six years old approaches
a foreign tourist. She wears jogging pants under an *anaku*
skirt, a *chumbi* woven belt, a faded Walt Disney T-shirt, and
a blue *chalina* wrapped around her shoulders. "*Regálame*"
(Give me a gift), she says, while extending her open hand. At a
busy intersection, a member of the Ecuadorian upper-middle
class encounters a young indigenous woman at his driver-side
window while he idles at a stoplight in his suv. "*Compre chicles*"
(Buy gum), the young woman says, with a few packets of gum
lodged between her fingers. Catching the driver's eye, she gives
a supplicating gesture and points to the toddler strapped to her
back: "*para el wawito*" (for the baby).

Since the mid-1990s rural indigenous women and children from the
central Andes have been migrating to beg and sell gum on the streets of Ecuador's largest cities. The majority of these women and children are from the
small, high-altitude community of Calhuasí, in the province of Tungurahua
(figure 2).[1] Begging and, more recently, selling gum have emerged as key means
to overcome diminishing agricultural returns and to meet rising cash demands
for basic necessities. No longer able to sustain themselves from the land alone,
by the mid-1990s women and children began to join the ranks of men in temporary out-migration. With few marketable skills and limited employment options, they turned to begging and quickly discovered it as a viable means of
earning income. Since then, begging has evolved to become more than merely a
survival strategy; it now intersects with conspicuous consumption, status, educational fulfillment, and the drive to be included in consumer culture.

While their overall numbers are small, these young women and children
are representative of much larger processes. Begging is a symbolically charged
activity. Their presence on the streets is a daily reminder of the poverty that

FIGURE 1. Selling gum in Quito. In the photo on the left, a twenty-eight-year-old woman sells gum with her nine-year-old son. In the photo on the right, a ten-year-old girl sells gum.

subsumes racialized minorities. They are emblematic of rural neglect and the decline of the small-scale agricultural sector, and representative of grave social and geographic unevenness. Yet beyond symbolism, women and children's involvement with begging is also counterintuitive. In a capitalist society where hard work is equated with development and begging is associated with decay, it is ironic that Calhuaseños have discovered begging as a path to progress.

This book explores the geographies of gender, race, ethnicity, and childhood within the context of both modernization and globalization. It is about the differentiated ways in which indigenous peoples are pulled into the modernization project. Isolated in the rural Andes, Calhuaseños have largely survived on subsistence-based agriculture until the last few decades. As a "free" indigenous community, or one that never belonged to a hacienda, external influences remained limited until the 1970s when nonindigenous outsiders began to trickle into the community for the first time. Because they subsisted largely outside of the market economy, the impact of economic globalization has had limited effects on Calhuasí. Their dire poverty is largely the product of a prolonged colonial history of racism and social exclusion rather than of the most recent phase of globalization. In recent years they have not become poorer; rather, they have become more acutely aware of their poverty.

FIGURE 2. Map of Ecuador.

The construction of Calhuasí's first road in 1992 may have been the key catalyst for recent social-spatial change. The new road provided not only an economic link to labor and commodity markets but also a way out for the community's young women and children, who formerly had been isolated at 11,150 feet (3,400 meters). Actively pulling themselves into the modernization process, young indigenous women and children have since been challenging their assigned positions in Ecuador's social and racial hierarchies. They are rejecting employment as domestic workers, striving for better education, and using their earnings to participate in consumer culture. To improve their economic positions they have shifted from agricultural work to informal street work. Rather than harvest potatoes on steep Andean slopes, they now harvest tourist dollars in the urban Gringopampa (Field of Gringos).

In this book, I aim to unravel myths surrounding the lives of young indigenous beggars, who are commonly misrepresented as "lazy Indians" and "juvenile delinquents." Defined within the modern construction of childhood, they are further perceived as innocent children exploited by "bad mothers." In this new construction, which has become hegemonic in the West, childhood is a period of dependence, vulnerability, and innocence. According to UNICEF (2004), "Childhood is the time for children to be in school and at play, to grow strong and confident with the love and encouragement of their family and an extended community of caring adults. It is a precious time in which children should live free from fear, safe from violence and protected from abuse and exploitation. As such, childhood means much more than just the space between birth and the attainment of adulthood. It refers to the state and condition of a child's life, to the quality of those years." For many of the world's children, this is a significant conceptual shift. Within this modern construction, children are no longer active producers but rather firmly placed within the world of school and play.

I also examine how indigenous youth's gendered, racialized, and ethnic identities shift between rural and urban spaces.[2] Indigenous children struggle with the vast incongruities between their lives and the lives they witness elsewhere. Yet children and youth in peripheral regions are not empty vessels who absorb modern notions of childhood to fit into imagined molds for the "global child." Rather, indigenous children and youth actively negotiate, traverse, embrace, and resist these constructs to weave their individual identities.

As Calhuasí's young people become increasingly engaged with the urban sphere, they are forced to negotiate their identities through everyday encounters with racism—a racism that inferiorizes Ecuador's indigenous peoples by ascribing both physical and cultural differences. By exploring race and ethnicity through the lens of childhood and youth, I bring attention to the fact that young people are situated at a vulnerable life stage where they must negotiate shifting and uncertain identity paths. They must traverse a vast geography of cultural, political, and economic influences, made all the more difficult for indigenous youth through formal schooling, migration, urban labor, television, changing notions of childhood, and a dissolving way of life. These youth are forced to engage with modernity in a way that is radically different from their parents. As a racialized and marginalized minority group, they face particular challenges.

This book is also about social and spatial distancing. Although begging is one of many street-level subsistence activities, it is often perceived as a particularly offensive one. In the current era of revanchism, a concept generally used in the context of North American and European cities, municipalities continue to redefine what is acceptable in public space. The term is derived from revanche—French for revenge—and, according to Neil Smith, the revanchist city "portends a vicious reaction against minorities, the working class, homeless people, the unemployed, women, gays and lesbians, [and] immigrants," brought on by a terror felt by middle- and upper-class whites (1996, 211). Revanchism is a vengeful, right-wing reaction against the supposed theft of the city. Smith explores this concept as it applies to Mayor Giuliani's zero-tolerance policies in New York City. Increasingly, cities across North America and Europe are also adopting similar punitive urban governance measures (Belina and Helms 2003; Bowling 1999; Hermer and Mosher 2002; Mitchell 1997; Smith 2002). Beggars are a target of this discourse, perceived to be at odds with the project for urban revitalization and landscape aesthetics (Mitchell 1997).

In Ecuador the situation is strikingly similar. In an example of how revanchism plays out in the South, I explore how street begging intersects with urban revitalization and the push for global tourism. I uncover how indigenous women and children are harassed and in some cases forcibly detained while municipalities attempt to control public spaces and sanitize the streets of the "*indio sucio*" (dirty Indian). I describe how beggars are depicted as offensive and disruptive to the image of a "Clean Quito" or the "Twenty-First-Century Guayaquil," as advocated by municipal campaigns. Even when selling gum, indigenous women and children are constructed as "disguised beggars" who "exchange misery for money"—thus broadening the definition of begging to exclude a wider range of street-level subsistence activities. Begging governance further relies on the dual discourses of "child saving" and "bad motherhood"—both of which are hedged in a racist subtext—as central justifications for removing indigenous beggars from the streets.

Given current political and socioeconomic conditions, the tapping of indigenous toddlers on driver-side windows is a reality that, despite the wishes of some, will not disappear simply by pushing these individuals back to the countryside. By exposing myths, this book aims to provide a more nuanced understanding of the reasons behind indigenous children and youth's involvement on the streets. It is a call to planners, policy makers, and social workers to consider the complex and varied factors that push marginalized families and children into begging. This book also veers from traditional scholarship in that it prioritizes the voices of children through a child-centered methodology. Children are rarely key informants of social inquiry and have for the most part remained marginalized in social analysis. Herein, children are socially significant protagonists.

Modernization Meets Globalization

The stories that unfold from this text provide a slightly different narrative on globalization. Undeniably, globalization has had a profound impact throughout much of the world. National economies are being integrated into an increasingly globalized political and economic system, facilitated through a recent intensification of time-space compression (Harvey 1990). Through new technologies, global communication grids, and international financial networks, globalization has left few corners of the world untouched. The effects of this intensification have been particularly significant in the Global South. Neoliberal structural adjustment programs (SAPs) have had devastating consequences for the world's poor while contributing to what some term the "globalization of poverty" (Chossudovsky 1997).

Research has demonstrated the often distressing effects of increasing globalization on marginalized children in nations of the periphery. Although these processes are certainly not uniform, in many regions of the Global South foreign debt and SAPs have had direct or indirect influence on children's mortality, access to health care, and nutrition (Bradshaw et al. 1993; Whiteford 1998). In some cases funding cuts have deteriorated education systems: while the costs of education have risen, classrooms remain overcrowded, resources limited, and facilities poor (Bonnet 1993). Faced with dire poverty, many children are often removed or kept out of school entirely to engage in caretaking, subsistence work, and/or paid employment (Dyson 2008; Katz 2001; Nieuwenhuys 1994; Onta-Bhatta 1997; Robson 1996). While many work at home in domestic or agricultural capacities, others migrate to urban centers in search of enhanced financial opportunities. The majority of these children end up working in the unregulated informal sector and/or on the streets (Beazley 1999; Hecht 1998; Kilbride, Suda, and Njeru 2000; Scheper-Hughes and Hoffman 1998). When I began this research, I too expected to find that increasing globalization and neoliberalization were the prime forces pushing indigenous children onto the streets. Yet I discovered that something different is happening in the community of Calhuasí.

This book provides a new twist on an old story: a tale of what happens when modernization meets globalization. Because it has subsisted largely outside of the dominant market economy, Calhuasí provides an example of a community where structural adjustment programs have had few measurable influences. In fact, with the construction of the community's first road in 1992, access to healthcare improved and more children are surviving now than ever before. Furthermore, education has not deteriorated in the community because it was *already* in very poor condition. If anything, educational conditions have been enhanced in the last ten years. For the community of Calhuasí, poverty has been a long-standing reality. As in the case of many of the nation's indigenous communities, this poverty is rooted in a colonial history and the well-entrenched processes of economic marginalization and social exclusion (see Larrea and North 1997). In fact, in a material sense community members have *not* become poorer during this most recent phase of globalization. Rather, because the road has enabled increased access to urban centers and facilitated greater access to goods, community members have actually become wealthier, at least as measured by the accumulation of material items. What has changed is that in the last ten years, they have developed a heightened sense of their poverty.

Global Export of Childhood

Calhuasí has not been immune from globalization in all of its varied forms. The global diffusion of social policy for instance has affected the community—particularly through the 1989 UN Convention on the Rights of the Child. On March 7, 1990, Ecuador ratified the UN convention—the first country in the Americas and the third country in the world to do so (MBS 2003). In 1991 the Foro por la Niñez y Adolescencia (Forum for Childhood and Adolescence) was created in an attempt to pressure the Ecuadorian government to uphold children's rights as entrenched in the UN convention. By 1998 several of these rights were written into Ecuador's constitution. A year later children's rights advocates and government agencies began working toward a new Ecuadorian civil code that would harmonize national law with the UN convention. In July 2003, thirteen years after Ecuador ratified the UN convention, the new Código de la Niñez y Adolescencia (Code of Childhood and Adolescence) came into effect. In the end the code was created with the input of over eighteen thousand individuals, including children, teens, professionals, and authorities (INNFA 2001). Being one of the last Latin American countries to create a national code of childhood, Ecuador now has one of the most advanced codes in the region.

The biggest struggle for this movement was to redefine children's rights according to a new philosophy referred to as the Doctrina de la Protección Integral (Integral Protection Doctrine). This is as opposed to the former approach, the Doctrina de la Situación Irregular (Irregular Situation Doctrine), which focused primarily on deviant and criminal minors, who were granted limited and loosely defined rights. Opponents criticized the old system for institutionalizing children, criminalizing children's poverty, and penalizing children like adults. The new approach, as incorporated into the 2003 Código de la Niñez y Adolescencia, recognizes the rights of all children and advocates for a more integrated, context-specific, child-centered approach to protecting children's rights (FNA 2001, 2002). Nevertheless, even though this doctrine is now entrenched in law, it has yet to be embraced by the majority.

Through international NGOs, media, and government agencies, these Western norms of childhood are now spreading throughout the nation. Posters and parades espouse the rights of the child. Brightly colored pictures of indigenous children are often at the forefront of these images. On June 1 the International Day of the Child is celebrated in Ecuador's urban parks, plazas, and shopping malls: races, clowns, face painting, and special store prices are the main events. How children interpret this day varies: Javier, a nine-year-old boy quoted in one of Quito's newspapers, said, "The Day of the Child is a celebration just for us. Because this is my day, I want my parents to buy me a really cool cell phone" (*La Hora* 2003). For children from Ecuador's marginalized rural areas, however, this day has little meaning.

As Sue Ruddick (2003) notes, the unfortunate reality is that as this modern construction of childhood is being exported to debt-ridden nations of the Global South, the resources needed to reproduce this idealized form of childhood are for the most part sadly lacking.[3] For low-income children, media representations of ideal childhoods portrayed through consumerist culture and television dramas may sharpen the experience of material poverty as one of inner deprivation (Stephens 1995). This is particularly true in Ecuador, where poverty rates are high and where the global discourse on childhood continues to gain ground. For Ecuador's elite, reproducing modern notions of childhood is not an issue: elite children live in gated communities, attend private schools, and play within the protected spaces of their private gardens. They have embraced the modern construction of childhood and have ample resources to reproduce it.[4] But for the majority of Ecuador's children, this is not the case.

Modern notions of childhood are infiltrating Calhuasí through NGOs, education, the media, and young people's experiences in the city. However, reproducing this idealized form of childhood is particularly problematic in indigenous communities because this modern construction is at odds with well-established understandings of childhood, parenthood, and caring.

Global Diffusion of Neoliberal Urbanism

The impact of globalization also shapes the lives of Calhuaseños on urban streets. In this case, it is through the increasing global diffusion of neoliberal urban policies. Currently, harsh neoliberal urban policies have diffused to Ecuador's largest cities, where conditions vary dramatically from those in the North. The cities of Quito and Guayaquil have recently initiated urban regeneration projects that seek to cleanse the streets of informal workers, beggars, and street children to project a sanitized, whitened image of the city. In fact, in 2002 the municipality of Guayaquil contracted former New York City police commissioner William Bratton to help shape the city's urban regeneration strategy (*El Universo* 2004a, 2004b). Bratton is well-known for coauthoring New York City's *Police Strategy No. 5* along with former mayor Rudolph Giuliani. Smith tellingly describes this document as the "founding statement of a fin-de-siècle American revanchism in the urban landscape" (1998, 2). Flown in from the United States, Bratton was paid close to thirty thousand dollars for three days of work—an astronomical wage by local standards. His diagnosis was an overhaul of Guayaquil's anticrime structure, which was later implemented under the name Plan Más Seguridad (Increased Security Plan) (*El Universo* 2004a, 2004b). This plan—referred to colloquially as Plan Bratton (2002)—was undertaken to "protect" the city's elite from the "dangerous" classes, including informal workers, beggars, and street children, who were seen to be overtaking the city.

Revanchism in Ecuador, however, is being implemented in a locally distinctive manner. It has become integrally linked to exclusionary discourses surrounding race, ethnicity, gender, and childhood. In this book I argue that Ecuador's particular twist on revanchism is through its more transparent engagement with the project of *blanqueamiento*, or whitening. Consequently, the nation's refinement of revanchist urban policies results in the displacement of racialized and marginalized individuals, thus forcing them into more difficult circumstances.

Fieldwork and Personal Politics

The stories within this text are based on in-depth fieldwork conducted between 2002 and 2006, including nineteen months of residency in Ecuador. This was a multisited research project, divided between Quito, Guayaquil, and Calhuasí. In total I conducted over 125 interviews. Despite my Quichua-language training, all interviews were conducted in Spanish. While Quichua is the first language of Calhuaseños, I discovered that their Spanish fluency was generally much better than my Quichua fluency. Thirty-seven of my interviews were with young women and children who beg in the city. Of these, the oldest was twenty-four years old and the youngest was seven. The average age was thirteen years old.

The remaining eighty-eight of my interviews were conducted with community members, indigenous leaders, teachers, politicians, academics, agronomists, social workers, religious leaders, urban planners, police officers, and government members, all of whom were connected to issues surrounding indigenous beggars. Of these individuals, thirty-five were indigenous (namely community members, indigenous leaders, teachers, and a few politicians and government members), while the remaining fifty-three were white-mestizo.[5] These interviews were complemented with participant observation and hundreds of field notes from informal conversations with indigenous women and children. While living in Calhuasí I also conducted a survey with forty-two children (in the fifth and sixth grades), concerning their work at home and in the city. My gatekeeper into the community was the Fundación Don Bosco, which is the only organization in Quito that works with indigenous migrants from Calhuasí.

Photography unexpectedly became a key part of my research methods. After each and every interview with young people, I took individual portraits as a token of reciprocity. Because I lived very close to a corner where many women and children from Calhuasí worked, I began to invite them to my apartment to rest, have some food, and look at these photographs. They would often come during the hottest part of the day to avoid the harsh effects of the equatorial sun. Eventually, young women and children came to visit me on a regular basis, often with the motive to collect photos or to look at photos that I had taken of their friends and family. By sitting together and conversing about these pictures, I learned so much more about the community. These visits became great moments to discuss their lives; in fact, some of my best interviews were conducted in my kitchen.

I have chosen to include a number of these photographs in this book. As some have commented, it may seem striking that so many of these children are smiling, given their life circumstances. This representation is in stark contrast to images we generally see of children from the Global South. The popular media often presents poor children as wide-eyed and suffering—images that are disturbing enough to force us to avert our gazes or, more generously, empty our pockets to provide donor aid (see Ruddick 2003). In this book I have made a strategic choice to present young people as smiling because I believe that this is how they would rather be portrayed. However, in doing so, I am in no way suggesting that the lives of these women and children are wonderful and that they love working as beggars. Quite the contrary: their lives are very difficult. However, although they may be materially poor, many of their life experiences are emotionally rich.

This book confronts numerous distressing and uncomfortable issues. Child poverty, begging, racism, and exclusion are not topics to be taken lightly. I take a particular stance, one which some may find controversial. After working and living with people from Calhuasí over the last seven years, I have come to believe that begging is a rational, legitimate, and even clever choice. Ecuador's indigenous peoples live in a highly racially stratified society. Indigenous peoples are positioned on the bottom rungs of the nation's racial hierarchy, which means that in practice they are accorded few rights in the city. But indigenous peoples have not endured this situation passively. Ecuador now has the strongest indigenous political movement in Latin America (see Becker 2008). However, there has been little substantive change in Ecuador's poorest indigenous communities, despite this active movement of resistance.

The reality remains that for indigenous peoples, particularly women, employment options are limited to highly gendered and racialized positions, such as domestic workers and dishwashers. While stigmatized, begging is an option that allows them to earn substantially more income than they could otherwise. It further allows them to work independently and on their own hours, while remaining the primary caretakers for their young children. Moreover, women are able to use their earnings to pay for their children's education, in the hopes that this will enable better and more prosperous futures.

This argument is in contradiction to many charities who advocate "no gift giving" in the belief that begging creates a pattern of dependency. This may be true in some instances, but in the case of Calhuasí's women and children, I disagree. In a society with no welfare system, begging may be perceived as an individual means of redistributing wealth among the poor. When charities step in to discourage begging or, rather, to encourage diverted-giving campaigns, they impose their value judgments on how the money should be spent and by whom. In my opinion, this is a rather paternalistic approach. Calhuasí's young indigenous women and children are very capable and do not need paternalistic organizations overseeing their spending. The majority have entered into begging as a rational strategy to earn income to help their children pursue their educational aspirations, to allow their families to build better homes, and to improve their material circumstances.

Some may dispute whether begging should be perceived as a legitimate form of employment, but I hope that this book will provide another side of the story: a story of how oppressed people use creative means to improve their life circumstances. I hope to demonstrate that begging is not destroying young people's lives (as some insist) but rather is enabling opportunities that the community's young people have never had before.

CHAPTER ONE

Ecuador

Economic Crisis, Poverty, and Indigenous Identities

We're lacking so much here. We've been left behind. So we're migrating.

—Baltazar, forty-one years old, Calhuasí, May 13, 2003

Political and Economic Crisis

In recent decades Ecuador has experienced vast change, along with an accelerated integration into the global economy. During this time the nation has been characterized by political instability, high income inequality, poverty, and massive debt. Between 1997 and 2007, seven presidents held office—three of whom were overthrown. Meanwhile, gaps between the rich and poor were among the highest in the world (Lind 2005). At the turn of the millennium, close to 60 percent of Ecuadorians lived in poverty, while this figure rose to almost 90 percent among indigenous peoples (SIISE 2003c). An astonishing nine out of ten indigenous Ecuadorians were unable to meet basic needs for food, housing, health services, and education.

Like elsewhere in Latin America, neoliberal restructuring has had a significant impact. Ecuador underwent its first round of structural adjustment programs (SAPS) in the early 1980s. Among other things, these led to currency devaluation, higher fuel prices, decreased subsidies for staple products, a switch to export-led growth, a rise in interest rates, and a reduction in government spending on health care, education, and social services (Weiss 1997). Ecuador's political and economic situation became particularly dire between 1995 and 1999. During this four-year period, the nation went to war with Peru, endured various government scandals, suffered a severe El Niño, and observed large-scale crop destruction. Falling world oil prices also beleaguered the nation, particularly since Ecuador's economy is largely supported by the export of Amazonian oil.

By 1999 Ecuador was in the midst of its worst economic crisis in recent history. In an attempt to curb rampant inflation and stabilize the economic situation, the government announced plans to abandon the national currency and adopt U.S. dollars in January 2000. Yet within three weeks of this controversial move, the president was overthrown by an indigenous- and military-led coup. Nevertheless, despite much popular opposition, dollarization proceeded in April 2000. This move drastically reduced real incomes for Ecuadorians. The local currency was fixed at 25,000 sucres to one U.S. dollar; four years prior it had been valued at 3,190 sucres to the dollar (Wibbelsman 2003). The immediate beneficial impacts of dollarization were limited: by 2001 Ecuador's per capita debt remained the highest in Latin America (Lind 2005).

The nation's neoliberal restructuring programs hit the agricultural sector particularly hard. For small-scale rural agriculturalists, many of whom are indigenous, neoliberal policies effectively blocked access to the key resources needed for continued agricultural production, resources such as land, credit, high quality seeds, and new technologies (Martínez Valle 2003). While the nation's neoliberal development policies have focused on large-scale, export-based agriculture (e.g., floriculture), the majority of small-scale rural agriculturalists have been left behind. Consequently, across the nation many indigenous farmers have abandoned their plots to pursue nonagricultural activities—most often in the urban informal sector (see Korovkin 1997).

As a result of high levels of rural poverty, Ecuador's streets are overwhelmed by poor people trying to make a living by selling anything and everything, including umbrellas, newspapers, bootlegged CDs, sunglasses, candies, and prepared foods. Young men ply their trades on buses and declare to passengers that they have decided to "earn an honest living selling candies rather than turn to a life of crime." Mothers board buses with sick children to implore assistance with medical costs. Children are ever visible on the urban streets as shoe shiners, candy vendors, flower sellers, entertainers, and beggars.

Ecuador's Indigenous Youth

At the turn of the millennium Ecuador claimed to have the highest rate of working children in all of Latin America (INNFA 2001). Although verifying this claim would be difficult, given the problems with collecting accurate data on child labor, the claim itself points to the issue's magnitude. Owing to higher levels of poverty among native people and considerable racial inequality, indigenous young people forge a significant portion of Ecuador's working youth.[1] Although the economic crisis has had a negative effect across Ecuador, the troubles have been particularly dire for indigenous children. For instance, in 1999, 60 percent of the nation's children lived in poverty. Yet the rates of poverty for indigenous youth were even worse: in the same year, a phenomenal 93 percent of rural indigenous children lived in poverty (SIISE 2003k). This figure becomes even more astounding when measured by indigence, defined as the inability to meet basic food needs: at the turn of the millennium, seven out of ten rural indigenous children were unable to meet basic food needs (2003j). By contrast, three out of ten rural nonindigenous children suffered the fate.

While the economic crisis has had a significant impact on Ecuador's indigenous youth, conditions for Ecuador's indigenous peoples have long been poor owing to a history of structural discrimination and social exclusion. For instance, life expectancy at birth for rural children living in provinces with high indigenous populations is consistently lower than for rural children elsewhere—in some cases by as much as eleven years (Poeschel-Renz 2003). Statistics from 1990 reveal that while the infant mortality rate for nonindigenous children was thirty for every one thousand live births, the rate for indigenous children during the same time period was fifty-six (Encalada, García, and Ivarsdotter 1999). Nutrition levels also show wide discrepancies. Nationwide, 24 percent of nonindigenous children suffer from chronic malnutrition, as compared with 58 percent of indigenous children (Larrea, Freire, and Lutter 2001).[2]

Despite the perceived value of education, increasing economic woes have further complicated indigenous children's access to school, particularly for girls. At the turn of the millennium, four out of ten indigenous girls had abandoned school to work in the city, at home, or in the fields. Across the nation, fewer than two in ten of all children had done the same (SIISE 2003o). Rural indigenous women above age twenty-four have an average of fewer than two years of schooling, compared with five years for rural nonindigenous women (2003g). These educational discrepancies are reflected in illiteracy rates: 53 percent of rural indigenous women are illiterate as compared with 17 percent of rural nonindigenous women. Meanwhile, across the nation, fewer than 11 percent of all Ecuadorians are illiterate (2003a).

Racism and Social Whitening

All of these larger socioeconomic changes are situated within the context of a prolonged colonial history of racism, social exclusion, and economic marginalization for Ecuador's indigenous peoples. Race is a social construction with no basis in biological reality, yet it continues to operate in the popular imagination as a powerful and exclusionary force (Wade 2002). Grounded in the "separation of human populations by some notion of stock or collective heredity of traits" (Anthias and Yuval-Davis 1992, 2), race establishes a contextual and relational boundary between those who can and cannot belong. In the Andes, race remains a social fact that naturalizes economic inequality. It is the basis for a social hierarchy that posits whites at the top and blacks and Indians at the bottom (Weismantel 2001, xxx).

Mestizaje is a core concept for discourses pertaining to race and ethnicity in the Andes. It is generally understood as a process of racial and cultural mixing, which involves the blending of Spanish, African, and indigenous ancestry. Yet there is a hierarchy in this mixture: those with more Spanish ancestry (or rather those who are whiter) are considered the pinnacle. Mestizaje is not only about physical whiteness but also about discursive whiteness. The ideology encourages individuals to gradually evolve from "primitive" Indianness into more "civilized" states of being—states that eventually become incompatible with indigenous ways (Bonnett 2000; de la Cadena 2000). At the same time, degrees of Indianness are partly measured by phenotypical markers such as "dark hair," "slanted eyes," and "less refined features" (Roitman 2004, 18). White skin and fair features are prized above all. Therefore, the process of mestizaje is not so much about mixing as it is about a progressive whitening of the population—often referred to as *blanqueamiento*. In fact, mothers who give birth to whiter children are often lauded for "improving the race." For this reason, scholars often use the term *blanco-mestizo* (white-mestizo) to refer to the dominant sector of society. Individuals within this sector are generally classed by wealthy elites as mestizo but self-identify as white (Whitten 2003).

Mestizaje and blanqueamiento are also strong cultural processes because there is an assumed malleability of race and ethnicity in the Andes. Referring to the construction of the Ecuadorian nation from 1930–1950, Kim Clark (1998, 203) states that "dominant ideology assumed that an Indian who learned Spanish, left behind his poncho and moved to the city would immediately begin to partake of national culture as a mestizo." This is well illustrated by the now widely cited words of former Ecuadorian president General Rodríguez Lara in 1972: "There is no more Indian problem. We all become white when we accept the goals of national culture" (Stutzman 1981, 45). In this view, the goals of national culture include building a white, westernized nation far removed from indigenous roots. If everyone is white-mestizo then the "Indian problem" disappears. What does this mean for indigenous beggars (who have not left behind their ponchos) on city streets? Are they a visible affront to the project of blanqueamiento? Do they betray the nation's Indianness to the modern world?

The importance of race and ethnicity in the Andes is best illustrated through a critical analysis of current Ecuadorian census figures. There is no clear consensus over the nation's ethnic and racial composition; these numbers depend largely on political positionings. Nevertheless, out of a total population of thirteen million, estimates suggest that approximately 40 to 65 percent of Ecuador's population is mestizo, 25 to 40 percent is indigenous, 3 to 10 percent is black, and 1 to 7 percent is white or "other" (CIA 2008; Halpern and Winddance Twine 2000; Wibbelsman 2003). Yet in the 2001 national census an overwhelming 77 percent of Ecuadorians self-identified as mestizo, 10 percent self-identified as white, 2.2 percent self-identified as black, 2.7 percent self-identified as mulatto, and a mere 6.8 percent self-identified as indigenous (SIISE 2003b). This latter number shocked many, particularly those involved with the indigenous movement. But these figures must be understood within the discourses of blanqueamiento and mestizaje. The following quote from an individual who participated in census data collection is illustrative: "We went to a home where they were clearly indigenous. . . . They were from Colta, Chimborazo [a renowned indigenous area] and were a large family. The father, mother, daughters, sons, daughters-in-law, sons-in-law, and grandchildren all lived in a big rented space. . . . The whole family was there and the father said, 'I'm mestizo. We're all mestizos'" (December 4, 2002).[3] According to the speaker, this man's indigenousness was defined by his community of origin, his large family, and perhaps his physical traits. In the speaker's mind he was "clearly indigenous." Nevertheless, this man chose to identify himself and his family as mestizo.

Ecuador's unexpected census results have been partially attributed to faulty methodology. The 2001 census contained six static "ethno-racial" categories from which individuals could choose: indigenous, black, mestizo, mulatto, white, or other. But these static categories failed to capture the fluidity of Andean racial and ethnic identities. During the census, self-identification may have been entirely relational to the enumerator's ethnic-racial identity. The census was also criticized because it presumed ethnic-racial homogeneity within families by asking one individual in each household—the "household head"— to speak for the entire family. Yet individuals within the same household may self-identify differently depending on variables such as age, gender, and education. Interviewing household heads (who are usually men) is problematic in and of itself, since racial and ethnic identity is more often defined by women (Clark 1998; Radcliffe 1999). Further problems with data collection are outlined by Karem Roitman (2004), who reveals that the enumerators were high school students, some of whom chose to skip the ethnic-racial identity question entirely. She speculates that enumerators may have believed the answer was self-evident (and filled in the answers themselves) or that ethnic and racial differences between the enumerators and the household members made them reluctant to even pose the question.

For many, self-identification as mestizo is an attempt to embrace the processes of mestizaje and to distance themselves from their indigenous roots. To be mestizo is to be Ecuadorian and thus belong to the national culture and society. On the other hand, a prolonged history of abuse in rural indigenous communities makes many remain suspicious of government representatives at their doors. An indigenous peer informed me that in his rural community of Peguche, families used to hide their valuables and children on census day. Under certain circumstances those who may otherwise self-identify as indigenous may choose to officially conceal their ethnic and racial identity as a way to avoid further discrimination and harassment. This may be because few benefits have ever come from being an Indian in the Andes.[4]

Space, Race, and Ethnicity in the Andes

In urban areas, mestizaje and blanqueamiento profoundly affect indigenous migrants. In Andean geographic imaginaries, there is a strict racial-spatial divide between rural and urban spaces. There is a belief that Indians and blacks belong in the rural zones whereas white-mestizos belong in the urban areas (Radcliffe and Westwood 1996; Rahier 1998). Whites and Indians are in fact often constructed in an oppositional binary; modernity and urban progress are associated with whiteness whereas backwardness and rural decay are associated with Indianness.

Andean geographic imaginaries are tied to romantic notions concerning indigenous peoples' connections to the earth, rural spaces, and agrarian life. Images circulated by tourist agencies depict rosy-cheeked, colorfully dressed indigenous men and women, smiling while working the land. These images suggest that "this is where they belong." These contrast with images of the downtrodden and misplaced Indian in the city, imagined to have lost his culture and his land. When Indians "invade" the city, as often suggested by contemporary newspaper articles (*El Comercio* 2002a), they disrupt popular geographic imaginaries and racial divides. Among white-mestizos, indigenous peoples' perceived association with the earth further reinforces their backwardness and inferiority. It stresses the distance from national urban culture and their presumed lack of civilization. It further incites a fear among white-mestizos of contamination from Indians' perceived proximity to mud and dirt (Orlove 1998).

In the Andes the exclusion of indigenous bodies from the urban sphere is often barely concealed through a form of hygienic racism (Colloredo-Mansfeld 1998). This hygienic racism stems from late nineteenth- and early twentieth-century discourses surrounding eugenics, biology, and disease (Capello 2005; Kingman 2006; Wilson 2004). Using these discourses, white elites from this period managed to rework the definition of urban space to exclude indigenous bodies from urban markets and streets. According to Fiona Wilson (2004, 178), they emphasized "a new semantic division between the uncivilized, disease-

ridden, ignorant Indian whose presence in town posed a threat to social order and the image of the honourable, respectable mestizo labouring classes
worthy of inclusion as subaltern citizens." Concerns over the spread of typhus
and smallpox were blamed on the "appalling ignorance of Indian women." Because of the elite's fear of contamination, municipal authorities and the church
concurred that Indians should be prevented from coming to town as much as
possible. Indigenous market women were perceived as particularly reprehen-
sible since "they were transgressing boundary lines—in the minds of the elite—
between town and country, health and disease, women's work and men's work,
and public and private space" (175). As I discuss later in this book, the infusion
of this hygienic racism into today's neoliberal urban strategies is a continuation
of this rhetoric.

Even though indigenous peoples are constructed as a contamination risk for
white-mestizos, it would seem that they too are subject to reciprocal contamination from urban influences. During a meeting I observed between municipal
authorities and social workers concerning indigenous migration and informal
work on the streets of Quito, an urban planner said, "They may arrive *sana*
[healthy] but they will leave *contaminated.*" A social worker reiterated, "We
want them to maintain their culture. We don't want them to become *contaminated*" (September 2, 2003).

These comments represent different exclusionary strategies but remap the
same spatial boundaries. In the Andes, clothing is a key marker of indigenous identity (Radcliffe 2000). For some, Nike baseball hats and Walt Disney
T-shirts, as increasingly worn and embraced by indigenous youth, are evidence
of the contaminating forces of the urban sphere. Others express much dismay
at the way urban influences are changing rural communities. Prior to my de-
parture from Ecuador, a peer wished to introduce me to an "authentic" indigenous community near Cayambe. We drove several hours on isolated dirt roads
to arrive at the community of Oyacachi. However, very dismayed with what she
saw, she said, "They never used to have electricity or tin roofs. . . . It was better before" (July 31, 2003). Her reaction is akin to what Renato Rosaldo (1989)
terms "imperialist nostalgia"—an innocent longing for an imagined past that is
complicit with fundamental inequality and domination.

Positioning Calhuasí

The community of Calhuasí fits into these romantic notions of indigenous
peoples.[5] It is a picturesque Andean community situated between 10,500 and
11,800 feet (3,200–3,600 meters) in altitude and surrounded by snow-capped
volcanoes. Calhuaseños are known for their brightly colored shawls, ponchos,

FIGURE 3. Three generations of indigenous community members from the village of Calhuasí.

and porkpie hats (figure 3). Although some outsiders would like to keep the village "intact" and "traditional," many community members—particularly young people—are desperate for change. Those who seek change are heading to the city to beg and sell on the streets in the hopes that these earnings will allow them to improve their material and social conditions.

The vast majority of indigenous women and children begging in Quito hail from the coupled villages of Calhuasí Chico and Calhuasí Grande (which I refer to simultaneously as Calhuasí unless otherwise specified; see figures 4 and 5). Located in the central Andean province of Tungurahua, Calhuasí Chico has a population of approximately 350 and Calhuasí Grande has a population of approximately 900 (figure 2). Until 1995 these two villages were politically united as one and thus remain very interconnected through marriages, schooling, land holdings, and community work projects. They are located in the upper, or Alto, zone of the rural civil parish (*parroquia*) of Quisapincha, approximately 93 miles (150 kilometers) from Quito or half a day's travel. There are six communities in Quisapincha Alto, all of which are Andean Quichua and belong to the Kisapincha ethnic group. All share similar geographies, histories, and socioeconomic conditions. The nearest city is Ambato (population of approximately

FIGURE 4. Looking south from Calhuasí Grande. The next ridge over is Calhuasí Chico, beyond which lies the village of Punguloma in the parish of Pasa. The inactive volcano Chimborazo (20,700 feet, or 6,310 meters) lies in the background.

FIGURE 5. Looking northwest from Calhuasí Grande over Quisapincha Alto. Villages include Illahua Chaupiloma, Illahua Grande, and Illahua Chico.

170,000) and is located 19 miles (31 kilometers) away. Despite Ambato's proximity, it can take up to two hours to reach the city owing to poor roads and steep Andean geography.

A smaller number of women and children who beg on the streets of Quito come from the surrounding high-altitude Kisapincha indigenous communities of Punguloma and Tilivi in the neighboring parish of Pasa (figure 4) and Illahua in Quisapincha Alto (figure 5), thus suggesting a regional trend. What distinguishes the Kisapincha from other indigenous communities in the Andes is women and children's involvement in begging. Other Andean indigenous women and children do engage in begging but do so almost exclusively at Christmas to capitalize on Christian charity. Calhuaseños, on the other hand, are engaged in begging year-round. Elsewhere in Ecuador temporary Andean migrations have also largely consisted of men (Lentz 1997; Sánchez-Parga 2002). Women and children's (particularly girls') involvement in temporary rural-to-urban migration is a relatively new trend, a trend that has accelerated since the mid-1990s.

Calhuasí has a different history than many indigenous communities in the Andes. It never belonged to a hacienda, which means that forebearers escaped the system of debt peonage or forced labor that wrought havoc on indigenous communities elsewhere. Although there are few written documents concerning the community's past, oral histories indicate that Calhuasí itself is fairly recent community, established during the postindependence or post-1822 period. As part of the Kisapincha ethnic group, the community formerly occupied the entire region surrounding and including the city of Ambato, which is now Ecuador's seventh largest city. Many community members still lay claim to areas of the city and have blood relatives (who now consider themselves nonindigenous mestizos) who live in the town of Quisapincha.

Oral histories suggest that the Kisapinchas moved into the mountains surrounding Ambato to protect themselves from the Spanish and Creole elite. Community members described how, until thirty years ago, guards were posted along Quisapincha Alto's narrow mountain ridges to watch the footpath for ascending intruders. If intruders were spotted, guards would blow on a long bamboo horn to alert the villagers. They would then roll boulders and stones down the mountain ridges to force the intruders back. Community members said they were hostile to outsiders because these they feared they would steal their land, children, and possessions. One man recounted his reaction when hearing the bamboo horn as a child: "Since we were just children, we were afraid. We cried. The elders would gather up pots, and anything [of value], and go up to the páramo, go hide in the mountains. They told us they were coming to steal children, they were coming to steal pots, and that, well, they were coming to take everything that we had" (May 28, 2003). Another man recounted that "Until 1975 the white man could not enter Quisapincha Alto. They could not enter. It was impossible" (May 4, 2003).

In 1938 Calhuasí was legally recognized as a *comuna* by the Ministry of Agriculture and Animal Husbandry. The Comuna Law came into effect in 1937, which means that Calhuasí was one of the first indigenous communities in Ecuador to be recognized by the government.[6] Because Calhuasí did not belong to a hacienda, community members already owned land when the land reforms of 1964 and 1973 came into effect. As a result, these national-level reforms had little impact on the community. Operating largely outside of the national market economy, Calhuasí remained a primarily subsistence-based economy until the 1990s. Lacking even a road until 1992, community members engaged in only periodic trade and barter in Ambato's and Quisapincha's local markets.

The construction of the road had a significant impact on the community and directly coincides with women and children's increasing rural-to-urban migration. Very little data is available for current socioeconomic conditions in Calhuasí; however, data exists that reflects the magnitude of impoverishment just prior to the construction of the road and into the late 1990s. For instance, in 1992 a full 83 percent of Calhuasí's men and 94 percent of its women were illiterate (CESA 1992). In 1994 nine out of ten children were malnourished (Cruz et al. 1994). Across Quisapincha Alto, seven out of ten children were either underweight or below average height as a result of malnutrition (1995). While the number of houses made of cement blocks has been increasing rapidly since the construction of the road, 70 percent of Calhuasí's houses were still made of mud and thatch in 1991 (Camacho Muñoz 1991). At the turn of the millennium, 84 percent of households had access to electricity in their homes and more than 90 percent had access to piped water, yet sewers, telephone lines, and medical services remained nonexistent.[7] The average life span was short across the communities: a mere 5 percent of the population was older than sixty. In contrast, the bulk of the population was young, with 52 percent younger than eighteen (COCIQ 1999).

Both Calhuasí Chico and Calhuasí Grande have bilingual (Spanish-Quichua) primary schools that include grades one through six, yet not one person has attained a high school education. Rather than attend high school, the majority of children leave school at age twelve to join the cash economy. While community members value education for their children, the quality of education is poor because of inadequately trained teachers, a lack of educational resources, poor school infrastructure, short school days, and frequent teacher absences. Attendance at the local high school is also made difficult owing to the poor quality of the road. Prior to the construction of the road, the only way in or out of the community was via a long and difficult footpath through the mountains. Even now, poor conditions cause the sixteen-kilometer journey to the parish center of Quisapincha to require a minimum of an hour and a half by car. The journey is also very dangerous; numerous trucks have plunged hundreds of feet down Quisapincha Alto's steep mountainsides.

Small-scale agriculture has traditionally been the economic mainstay for the community. Although steeply sloped, the land is covered in a deep volcanic soil that is rich in organic content (CESA 2002). Popular crops in the region include potatoes, *haba* beans, barley, wheat, and Andean root crops such as *mellocas*, *mashua*, and ocas.[8] Community members insist that, even though the land is fertile, they can no longer subsist from agriculture alone. There are several complicating factors that have led to this predicament, including increasing intensity of land use and land fragmentation, declining agricultural returns, and the rising need for cash income.

The community's population has grown significantly in recent years: estimates for rural Quisapincha suggest an annual growth rate of 6.3 percent (COCIQ 1999).[9] Without birth control, women continue to have children throughout their reproductive years. High infant mortality rates have traditionally kept population numbers low. In 1957 the infant mortality rate for the entire parish of Quisapincha was 547 children for every 1,000 births. In the same year, the infant mortality rate for Ambato was 95 children for every 1,000 births (Peña-herrera de Costales, Costales Samaniego, and Bucheli 1961). I spoke to one Calhuaseño couple that had lost 7 of their 11 children. The father explained, "They were illnesses that we didn't know at the time. In that time there was no doctor in Quisapincha. And we couldn't get there [Quisapincha] either and well, there was no medical center. I mean, there weren't cars like there are now. Nor was there a road. And the footpath down was very difficult" (April 27, 2003). But with the introduction of the road, they now have better access to medical care and basic vaccines and, consequently, more children (and adults) are living. Community members have mixed feelings about this: one thirty-four-year-old woman bemoaned how unlucky she was that all six of her children had *lived*. In the context of high infant mortality rates, women from the community have perhaps developed an ethic of "indifference to death" as an emotional tactic to cope with poverty and recurrent death. It is a mother's love that has been shaped by harsh economic, social, and cultural constraints. In her analysis of poor Brazilian women, Nancy Scheper-Hughes (1992) refers to this as "death without weeping"—a forced detachment from personal tragedy that allows women to get by in the face of frequent emotional trauma.

Higher overall population has resulted in increasing land pressure. There is a tradition of land inheritance in the community, which fragments the land into smaller and smaller parcels. Agricultural plots are used intensively year-round without any fallow periods. Community members can produce only a small amount of food on their parcels, often just enough for subsistence needs. When Calhuasí's population was lower, agricultural plots concentrated in the more fertile valleys. In search of further land, Calhuaseños push into the region's steep slopes and into the páramo—the environmentally sensitive land above 11,500 feet (3,500 meters). When used for grazing cattle and growing potatoes, the lands of the páramo quickly become eroded, compacted, and infertile. Because the páramo is the source of the entire region's water (supplying almost forty thousand users in and around Ambato), this trend will present significant environmental (and political) problems in the years to come (CESA 2002). Erosion is also a problem for the majority of cultivated lands. Very steep grades and little terracing allow heavy rains to wash away topsoil year after year. An agronomist from Tungurahua's Ministry of Agriculture predicts that if current land-use patterns continue, the future productivity of the land will be short lived (May 28, 2003).

As Calhuasí becomes more integrated into the market economy, agricultural prices are also a significant problem. Even though community members were primarily engaged in subsistence production, they were able to sell some goods in exchange for basic food staples, livestock, and agricultural supplies. But since the economic crisis and subsequent dollarization brought severe inflation, the costs of supplies, such as fertilizers, fungicides, and veterinary medicines, have become elevated.[10] Meanwhile, a regional flooding of the market by cheaper agricultural imports from Colombia and Peru has caused prices to drop. In 2001 and 2002 a quintal of potatoes sold for between fifty cents to one dollar.[11] A parcel of land generally produces ten to fifteen quintals of potatoes. Therefore, even if community members sold their entire harvest, they would earn a dismal five to fifteen dollars for six to eight months of labor. Their increasing integration into the market economy has reinforced the need for cash income. After explaining this situation to me, one community member exclaimed, "For one dollar, you can't even buy a large cola! Where are we supposed to get the money?" (May 13, 2003). In the opinion of an employee from Tungurahua's Ministry of Social Welfare, agricultural merchants are the winners, while rural agriculturalists barely scrape by: "Merchants practically rob them. They lose in ingredients; they lose in labor; they lose in time. . . . It's really difficult—with earnings around four or five dollars after six months of work they really can't survive. So this situation forces them to leave" (June 3, 2003).

Calhuaseños have not sat passively by during this period of rapid socio-economic change. Inspired by Ecuador's powerful indigenous political movement, Calhuaseños have become more politically active. For instance, during Ecuador's 1992 indigenous uprising, they reappropriated lands in the town of Quisapincha that had been seized by the church. On this land they built a political office for the Confederación de Organizaciones Campesinas Indígenas de Quisapincha (Confederation of Indigenous Peasant Organizations in Quisapincha), which now advocates for the rights of the Kisapincha. In 1997 community members from across Quisapincha Alto successfully mobilized to have an indigenous leader from Illahua Chico elected as the parish political lieutenant, or *teniente político* (COCIQ 1999). Yet after seven months in office, opposing white-mestizos forced him out. Since then at least two more indigenous leaders have been elected (one from Calhuasí Grande in 2000 and one from Illahua Grande in 2003). While relations are improving between the Kisapincha and local white-mestizos, Kisapincha indigenous leaders continue to face much opposition from the townspeople. As a result, local indigenous activists have yet to make significant socioeconomic gains for the communities of Quisapincha Alto.

Rural-to-Urban Migration

When Calhuasí's women and children migrate to the city, they go for a minimum of four days to a maximum of two months. There is a seasonality to this migration: they tend to migrate over long weekends, school holidays, or during teachers' strikes (which were quite frequent at the time of this research). They migrate as family units and work together on the streets as part of tightly knit kinship groups. Men sometimes come to the city as well, but rather than work as beggars or vendors they generally work as shoe shiners. Dominant Ecuadorian gender ideologies prevent the majority of men from begging. The only exceptions include elderly men, disabled men, young boys, or boys carrying babies. These dominant gender ideologies dictate that able-bodied adult males are simply unsuccessful on the streets in their requests for charity. However, more often than not, men stay behind in the countryside to take care of the animals and any children that have remained at home.

The majority of migrating families have worked in both Quito and Guayaquil, Ecuador's two largest cities. This research primarily focuses on the capital of Quito, although chapter 5 does present some comparative data from the coastal city of Guayaquil (figure 2). Quito is situated high in the Andean sierra at 9,200 feet (2,800 meters) and has a population of more than 1.8 million people. Slightly south of the equator, the city occupies a long, narrow valley surrounded by volcanoes. The majority of Calhuaseño men, women, and children work in the more prosperous north end of the city, where new developments continue to sprout. From Parque el Ejido northward, they work the main intersections along the trolley lines of Avenida Seis de Diciembre and Avenida Diez de Agosto, in the backpackers' district (Gringopampa) near Avenida Río Amazonas, and in the international oil district near Avenida Portugal (figure 6).

At intersections, they spend eleven hours a day selling gum and/or begging from Quiteños prosperous enough to own cars. In the oil district, in the backpackers' district, and outside of the international airport, they occupy sidewalks—sometimes sitting and sometimes standing. Children below the age of fourteen rarely work alone and almost always work with or within viewing distance of a teen or an adult extended family member.

When asked why they migrate to the city, they almost always respond, "*No tenemos dinero*" (We don't have any money). As Ecuador becomes increasingly integrated into the market economy, the need for cash is reinforced. Calhuaseños can no longer be self-sufficient because they cannot produce some of the basic staples they have learned to depend on, such as white rice, oil, sugar, flour, pasta, and salt. White rice in particular is a fairly new introduction to the diet. As recently as 1993, the main staples of their diet were recorded as being barley, potatoes, and Andean root crops (Chango 1993). From my experience living in the community, white rice now constitutes the bulk of every meal. According to an indigenous woman who works with Calhuaseños in the city, "They say that they come [to the city] because their crops take too long to mature and they never get a fair price for their products. They pay them very little. . . . Even though they have grains and potatoes, they don't have salt; they don't have lard. You need money for these things . . . and there's no way of making it in the community. So, they have to come to the city, even if it is to beg. And when they beg, people give them money so they keep coming back" (August 26, 2003).

While often driven by economic motives, there are many other factors that play into migration. Feminist and postcolonial research has demonstrated that women in particular often have multiple motivations for migrating, some of which are influenced by household power dynamics, domestic disharmony, and dominant representations of family, morality, and sexuality (see Silvey and Lawson 1999; Silvey 2004; Willis and Yeoh 2000). Women are also pushed to the city because they increasingly require cash to pay for their children's school supplies, which include uniforms, notebooks, and school lunches. As the community itself becomes more integrated with the urban sphere and Western culture, Calhuaseños are being exposed to alluring consumer commodities. The draw of consumer culture is strong and they most certainly want a part of it.

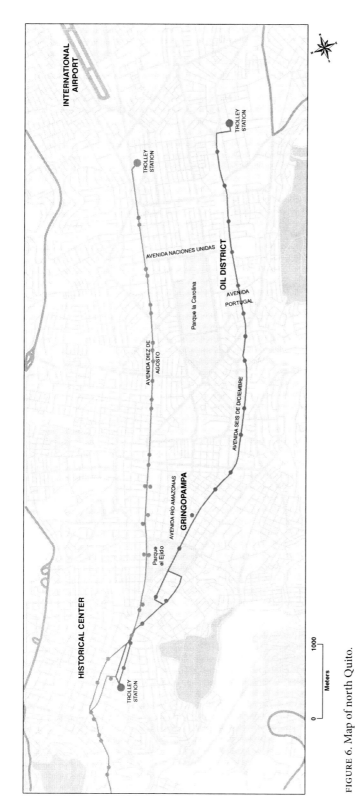

FIGURE 6. Map of north Quito.

Commodities such as portable stereos, televisions, trucks, cell phones, bicycles, blenders, and name-brand clothes are coveted goods in the community. Yet the number of individuals owning consumer goods remains low. As stated by the president of one of the community's newly formed organizations, "We're lacking so much here. We've been left behind. So we're migrating" (May 13, 2003). Community members no longer want to be left behind, and begging is a strategy that, perhaps ironically, is allowing them to move ahead.

CHAPTER TWO

Indigenous Childhoods

Gender, Work, Education, and
Migration in the Andes

The children and youth who are leaving the community, they're different. They're not like before.
——Nadia, thirty-four years old, Calhuasí, April 27, 2003

Conditions are changing for indigenous children in Ecuador, particularly for young people in Calhuasí. These changes are being brought about for several reasons, but one of the more significant is the reconceptualization of local understandings of childhood. It is now widely recognized that constructions of childhood are socially, culturally, and historically specific (Aitken 2001; Ariès 1962; James and Prout 1997; Holloway and Valentine 2000). Yet in recent years the modern Western construction of childhood has infiltrated Ecuador's indigenous communities through education, media, and rural-to-urban migration. The result is that local understandings are being displaced in favor of this new modern ideal. Gender constructs are also changing as community members become exposed to new gender norms. Whereas the Andean indigenous household was once regarded as the "two-headed household" because of a fairly equitable distribution of resources and labor (Hamilton 1998), community members are now experiencing a shift to less equitable gender norms.

Consequently, children and adults are experiencing much conflict as they try to negotiate these new identity paths. This process is all the more fraught for youth—particularly indigenous youth—who are involved in a complex process of identity formation. As aptly stated by Blanca Muratorio (1998, 411) regarding Quichua girls in the Ecuadorian Amazon, "To deal with the experiences of selfhood, they must walk through the uncertain and shifting boundaries of at least three main identity paths: the contested one already traveled by their elders, the glamorous and appealing one drawn by the mass media and shared with their peers, and the politically compelling one offered by indigenous organizations."

These are not easy choices. Indigenous youth are placed at a nexus of conflicting and overlapping pulls that increasingly set them apart from past generations. Through formal schooling, migration, urban labor, television, changing notions of childhood, and a dissolving way of life, these youth are forced to engage with modernity in ways that are radically different from their parents.

In this chapter, I trace how childhood, gender, work, education, and migration are restructuring young indigenous lives. I explore shifting patterns in work, problems with education, youth aspirations, young women's migration, and gender and sexuality. In doing so, I try to uncover the main factors affecting young Calhuaseños' lives and unravel how some of these factors are influencing youth migration into the cities and onto the streets.

Childhood, Gender, and Work

In the Global North, the vast majority of young people experience childhoods that correspond to the dominant Western construction; that is, childhood is understood as a time for play, innocence, and learning. Of course, there are exceptions but for the most part the experience of childhood in the Global North is at tremendous odds with the experience of childhood in the Global South. In this new Western construction, "Children have become relatively worthless economically to their parents, but priceless in terms of their psychological worth" (Scheper-Hughes and Sargent 1998, 12). Globalization has intensified the export of this Western-based ideal through the media, NGOs, and international conventions, such as the UN Convention on the Rights of the Child. Yet in many parts of the world high levels of poverty and structural inequality prevent this construction from being reproduced. Further impeding its adoption is the reality that this hegemonic Western construction is often at odds with local preexisting ideologies.

In Ecuador this is precisely the case. Indigenous rights activists have taken issue with the UN Convention on the Rights of the Child, a document that espouses the dominant Western construction of childhood and that has now been ratified by the vast majority of the world's nations. The UN convention defines a "child" as anyone under the age of eighteen. However, in the indigenous construction of childhood, maturation is dependent on an individual's level of responsibility (Tibán 2001). As explained by an indigenous university lecturer, "In the Andean world, we usually joke that up to four years of age, you get to live for free. From the age of four onwards, little ones know how to take animals to pasture; at six, they already know how to cook; at eight or ten years of age, they can pretty much work the land; at the age of ten to twelve, they can harvest. . . . So by the age of fourteen or fifteen, we are experts in the indigenous way of life" (August 1, 2003). Indigenous activists argue that work contributes to the reproduction of community values and to children's socialization, education, identity formation, recreation, and preparation for adult life (Tibán 2001). They argue that the UN convention ignores the important role that work has in their communities.

In 2003 Ecuador built on the UN Convention on the Rights of the Child to create its own national Code of Childhood and Adolescence. After much debate and consultation, this code incorporated indigenous concerns. Article 86 of the code provides a special exception for "formative cultural work." If work transmits "cultural norms and values," children under age fifteen may work, providing this work respects their "physical and psychological development" (MBS 2003). While defining children's work as "cultural" risks naturalizing children's involvement in work as a cultural choice rather than an economic necessity (Martínez Novo 2006), children have been in involved in formative rural labor for hundreds of years.

The *First New Chronicle and Good Government*, a 1,200-page manuscript written in 1615, depicts life in the Incan Empire before and after the Spanish Conquest. It details children's work as divided by age and gender. Five hundred years ago, children between ages five and eighteen were expected to pasture llamas and alpacas, work in the fields, gather firewood, weave, cook, clean, collect plants, make chicha, and care for younger children (Guamán Poma de Ayala and Frye 2006). Like elsewhere in the world, children in rural areas contributed vast amounts of their labor to households and agricultural systems. Children's work was an integral part of community life.

While children's labor remains limited in the Global North, in indigenous communities children's involvement in rural labor remains a central tenet of indigenous life. The words of an indigenous political leader express this clearly: "The indigenous way of thinking . . . is that a child has to work. In indigenous areas, you will not find a mother working without a child working alongside, pulling along a cow. . . . You will not find a child that cannot collect plants for the guinea pigs or for the rabbits. That the child should work is a way of thinking. From a very young age, they become involved with the land, with Allpa Mama [Mother Earth]." This labor not only is part of a way of life, but it contributes to the formation of children's environmental knowledge—knowledge that is crucial to their presumed agrarian futures. She continued, "In the community, we see those little jobs that children do as something dynamic that has to do with life. . . . At six years of age, for example, children lead cattle, give them water, bring them to the lake to drink, [and] peg them down so they graze only in a small area. . . . They already know how to collect plants. Because a six-year-old child who doesn't know how to collect plants—how will he live? How will he deal with his reality?" (August 5, 2003) To succeed and prepare for this reality, children must learn how to work at a young age.

In Calhuasí individuals are considered more or less capable of heading a household by age ten. By this point in life they have learned everything they need to know to live on their own. Their training begins when they are young; children begin helping with dishes, cooking, and cleaning when approximately four years old. As time progresses, "Children continue to learn with each thing they do. . . . If we start washing, they start washing. When we're working, they also want to work. When we're collecting plants, they also want to collect plants. So with every activity we do, they also do and in this way they learn many things" (April 27, 2003). In the early stages of this research, I was surprised when two twelve-year-old girls prepared a meal over an open fire for approximately seventy individuals. But after living in the community, I realized that this is not unusual by community standards. This realization was especially reinforced after an eight-year-old boy, in his mother's absence, cooked my lunch.

Indigenous children's work has traditionally integrated many aspects of play—play that often helps them learn and master new skills. This has been well documented elsewhere by Cindi Katz (1991, 2004) in Sudan and by Samantha Punch (2003) in Bolivia. Katz (2004, 60) states, "An element of play was almost fused with the work of children—they worked at play and they played at work—temporally, metaphorically, and imaginatively." In Calhuasí, work is not always separated from play. While collecting plants, Nicola made a hat out of reeds. While watching over grazing sheep, Alejandro and his siblings turned it into a game. As they ran around with squeals of laughter, the eldest played the shepherd, the second eldest played the wolf, and the youngest children played the sheep. On the way to pasture, I observed a six-year-old boy ride happily on the back of a pig while herding the rest of the animals with his stick. While returning home from harvesting potatoes at their grandparents' house, Flora and Pablo took turns riding down a hill in a wheelbarrow. By actively observing and playfully imitating their parents and siblings, children learn important knowledge and reproduce cultural behavior.

Because work is such an important component of rural agrarian life, indigenous children's value has traditionally been measured by their utility. James and Linda Belote (1984, 37) record an interesting anecdote from their research with the Quichua Saraguros in southern Ecuador: "It has been more than forty days since she gave birth to Vicente, so Balbina is now able to leave the house and attend mass. We meet her on the street and she has Vicente with her. Vicente is swaddled and wrapped, but we can see his face. 'What a beautiful child,' Linda comments. 'Oh, but he is completely useless. All he can do is eat and dirty his clothes.'" Being viewed as useful and productive has long been key to success in rural communities. From a very young age, children are taught the importance of being hard workers. As stated by one indigenous leader, "From the moment a child begins to crawl, from the moment he begins to take his first steps, his level of participation in family activities is measured by degrees. The child that works is perceived well. If a child attempts to grasp a hoe even though he's not yet capable, we believe that this child will be a good worker" (August 5, 2003).

Being lazy is particularly criticized. An Andean credo, one that has been adopted by the indigenous movement, is *ama killa; ama llulla; ama shua* (don't be lazy; don't lie; don't steal). The indigenous leader continued, "In the indigenous worldview, a child that does not show much ability during his first six years . . . we believe that this child will end up being lazy." A lazy child is a "spoiled child with no chance at a good future." In her opinion, a lazy child will "be defeated in life" (August 5, 2003). This may be why, in an open-ended survey question, 14 percent of the children in Calhuasí wrote that of all the things they do, "play" is their least favorite activity. These were children between the ages of eleven and fourteen. When asked why, they wrote, "Because I like to work." Another 21 percent of children wrote that of all the things they do, they like to work in agriculture the most. When asked why, an eleven-year-old girl wrote, "because I like to work hard"; a twelve-year-old boy wrote, "because I like to help my family"; another wrote, "because I like to eat." Seven percent of children explicitly wrote that of all the things they do, being "lazy" is their least favorite. One wrote that he does not like to be lazy because he wants to be "a good person." Being known as a hard worker remains crucial in Calhuasí. When I conveyed these sentiments to ten-year-old Nicola and told her that some of her older peers said that "play" is their least favorite activity, she said, "That's a lie. All children like to play" (March 17, 2003). But whether or not these children are lying is not the issue. Rather, their responses reveal the importance of a strong work ethic in Calhuasí. Community social pressures reward hard workers and push children to act accordingly.

In contrast to the rest of Ecuador, the gendered division of labor is fairly equal among children in Andean indigenous communities. My survey results reveal that between the ages of eleven and fourteen, boys and girls in Calhuasí work an average of five to six hours a day on agricultural and domestic chores. As evident from figure 7, the total hours worked differs little by age and gender. This gender-based distribution of labor tends to carry over into resource allocation; for the most part men and women have shared control over economic resources and equal say in decision making. Land inheritance practices favor male and female siblings equally, which means that the majority of women own land independently of their husbands (Hamilton 1998). Women do tend to specialize in domestic work; however, men's involvement in child care, cooking,

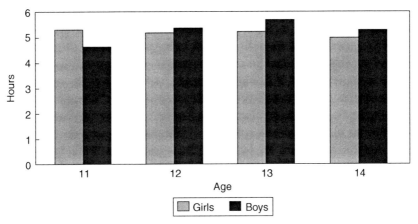

FIGURE 7. Hours worked per day by age and gender.

and laundry is not at all unusual. As figure 8 reveals, boys in Calhuasí are involved in cooking, washing, cleaning, and caretaking at a level that is almost
equal with girls.

In Calhuasí boys and girls are involved in a range of labor activities. Domes-
tically, children cook, wash dishes and clothes, clean, collect water, collect firewood, and care for younger siblings. Agriculturally, children help prepare the
land, plant crops, weed, irrigate, cultivate crops, and apply pesticides. Children
are also responsible for bringing animals to pasture, collecting food for animals,
fetching water and firewood, and killing guinea pigs, rabbits, and chickens (figures 8, 9, and 10). At present there are only slight gender-based variations in the
distribution of labor across domestic, agricultural, and shepherding activities.

Yet gender roles are shifting as community members become exposed to less
egalitarian gender constructs. Through migration, education, and the media,
new ideologies are infiltrating the community and exposing young people to
alternative modes of thinking. Meanwhile, economic pressures have accelerated because of an increasing demand for material goods and the markers of
"progress" (such as televisions, DVD players, and trucks). The rising importance
of education is also pushing families to earn cash income to pay for their children's schooling in the hopes of bettering their futures. As a result, children's
work is changing. According to an indigenous lecturer, "The education that
we used to receive was by imitation. When we were kids we would play while
imitating our parents' activities. So these games served to prepare us for our
future jobs. But obviously now, this work that I'm describing as play, we need to
take this work more seriously. Because when our parents migrate to the cities
to look for money, this work becomes much more serious, whether it be taking

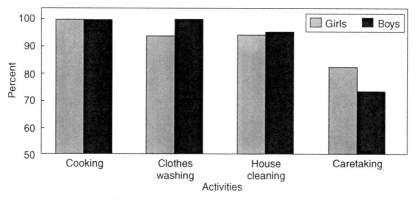

FIGURE 8. Percentage of children engaged in domestic activities.

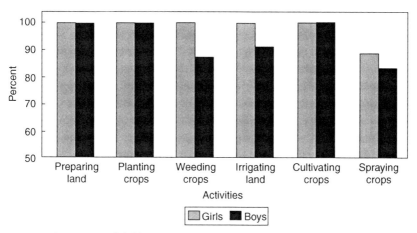

FIGURE 9. Percentage of children engaged in agricultural activities.

care of the animals, or doing domestic work, or cooking food, or doing handicrafts, or agricultural work. So from a very young age onward, what used to be play becomes very serious work" (December 18, 2002). As stated by fourteen-year-old Malena, "We don't play in rural areas. All we do is work. We work like donkeys [*burros*] but we don't make any money. We have to work if we want to eat" (August 21, 2003).

In a world where cash demands are high and children's work is the norm, families do not hesitate to incorporate their children into urban work. As a result, children are caught between competing discourses. On the one hand, economic pressures and cultural norms insist that they need to work; on the other,

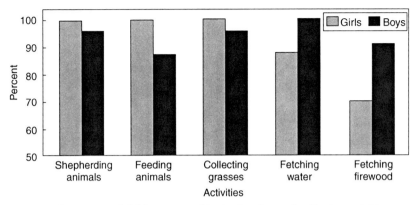

FIGURE 10. Percentage of children engaged in shepherding and collecting activities.

educators and the media dictate that they need to play and study. These competing discourses are also having an impact on some of the community's adults. Calhuasí's kindergarten teacher, a local thirty-four-year-old woman, spoke to this issue: "In the old days, more in ancient times when, as they say, there was a lack of civilization . . . they pushed children harder. Before there wasn't, like they say now, much care for children. But now we know that we shouldn't mistreat children. Now, we're not like our ancestors before. They wanted children to work like adults. But we, and those people who are in the know, we're learning a lot. So we don't do this. We want them to keep studying. That's what we're doing. We don't force our children [to work]" (April 27, 2003). This quote is profoundly illustrative of the ongoing changes concerning constructions of childhood in the community. As of yet her words do not reflect the views of many, but because she is an outspoken community leader, her influence in the community is great. Her words reveal how the modern construction of childhood has influenced her way of thinking. She speaks almost as if she has found a new religion, as she describes their former ways. Education is having a profound impact on these changes.

Childhood, Gender, and Education

Calhuasí's first school was built in 1975. It was a one-room schoolhouse run by an evangelical missionary. During the school's early years, enrollment rates remained low as parents approached this new institution with caution. The education children received was in Spanish, a language previously spoken only outside of the community; however, in 1988 the Ecuadorian government instituted a national bilingual education system available to indigenous communities that requested it. By the early 1990s attendance at the primary school had grown to more than 130 students; these students were packed into two small classrooms and instructed by a mere three teachers. In an attempt to acquire more teachers and better resources, the community petitioned for the Spanish-Quichua bilingual system in the early 1990s. In 1996 they were successful and received five new teachers for Calhuasí Grande, three new teachers for Calhuasí Chico, and funds for more classrooms.

While education has improved since the bilingual education system was introduced, the state of the facilities and the quality of education are poor at best. In fact, children who graduate from sixth grade are often unable to read properly. An indigenous nun who works in the community blames this on poorly qualified teachers, some of whom have not even graduated from high school themselves. Owing to a shortage of teachers fluent in both Spanish and Quichua, all but one of Calhuasí's teachers are from other provinces in the central Andes. When given the chance to work in their home provinces, most leave Calhuasí immediately, a fact that has led to a high rate of teacher turnover. Many parents and students complain of teachers' use of corporal punishment. I met at least two students who had been withdrawn from classes after excessive abuse in the classroom. Because of bad weather (which makes the roads impassable) and teacher strikes (from low pay and poor working conditions), classes are frequently cancelled. Other events lead to class cancellation as well: during the month that I lived in Calhuasí, classes were cancelled every Friday so teachers could play soccer with their peers. I also discovered that teachers often arrive late and leave early (frequently because of bad roads), thus reducing class time from the scheduled five hours to sometimes no more than three hours. Furthermore, the state of the classrooms themselves is abysmal, with broken windows and desks (figure 11).

The poor state of education affects the few children who do continue on to high school. There is an elevated rate of failure among youth from Calhuasí who attend the local high school in Quisapincha. For instance, between 1995 and 1999 an average of 7.6 percent high school students failed a grade in the Ecuadorian sierra (SIISE 2003p). Yet among students from Calhuasí, 22 percent failed in the 2002–2003 school year and 44 percent of students either failed a grade or failed one or more of their courses. This elevated failure rate reflects the low level of educational training available in the community.

There has been much criticism of Ecuador's bilingual education system. Critics claim it is underfunded, lacks proper educational resources, and hires teachers that are poorly trained. An indigenous university lecturer criticized the system for relying on nonindigenous models of education. In his opinion,

FIGURE 11. Children gathered (and giggling) at a broken classroom window.

this system "kills culture." He also believes that current models of education are distorting traditional gender roles and creating a "terrible divide" in indigenous families, wherein girls are relegated to the private sphere and boys to the public (August 1, 2003).

This new divide is depicted in tables 1 and 2, which reflect the job aspirations of boys and girls in Calhuasí. In Calhuasí Grande, the fifth- and sixth-grade teacher put forth a few occupational suggestions while I was conducting the survey—suggestions that reflect a profound imposition of gender and class constructs. In his mind, girls could become housewives or secretaries and boys could become mechanics. The survey results reveal the power of suggestion (table 1). In Calhuasí Chico, the teacher refrained from making suggestions and, consequently, responses do not reflect the same level of gender differentiation (table 2). Even though Calhuasí Grande's teacher is an indigenous man from the province of Chimborazo, he too has been trained within the confines of Ecuador's dominant model of education. In his teaching, he imposes this model and its corresponding constructs.

External pressures on the community have influenced many parents to emulate gender models that place priority on boys' education. For instance, in

Table 1 Calhuasí Grande student aspirations

#	Boys	#	Girls
8	Mechanics	5	Secretaries
3	Police officers	2	Housewives
1	Security guard	1	Treasurer
1	Soldier	1	Mechanic*
1	Teacher		

* One twelve-year-old girl wrote that she wants to be a mechanic, but I suspect she copied from one of her male peers. When I interviewed her later, she told me that she wants to be a teacher.

Table 2 Calhuasí Chico student aspirations

#	Boys	#	Girls
4	Teachers	5	Tailors
2	Tailors	4	Teachers
2	Masons	1	Housewife
1	Doctor		

Calhuasí girls are much more likely to be withdrawn from school and put into the rural or urban labor force than boys. In my sample of thirty-seven working children from Calhuasí, all seventeen boys, or 100 percent, had completed sixth grade or were continuing their education. Out of twenty girls, 11 or 55 percent had completed sixth grade or were currently enrolled in high school. Nine girls, or 45 percent, had been withdrawn from school or had never attended school at all. When asked, girls explained that they had no money for school supplies or that their mothers needed their help at home. Young girls are also more likely to be enrolled in school at a later age than boys. Before they enroll, many work for a few years to save up for school or to help support their siblings' education. According to Calhuasí's fifth- and sixth-grade teacher (the same teacher who influenced the previously mentioned results), many girls drop out or enroll late because parents believe that "Girls don't need to be in school so much. Rather they need to be at home so they can help take care of children, so they can help with agricultural work. And when the parents go to the city, it's better if [girls] stay to replace the parents. . . . So because of this, there are few girls in school. On the other hand, for boys, I think parents place a bit of priority on boys. They say that [boys] need to finish school because men will make something out of their lives. For women, they don't really give them much importance" (April 22, 2003). However, I suspect that the teacher's words represent his personal beliefs rather than those of the majority of parents.

While gender ideologies do play a role, girls are also withdrawn from school because they can earn significantly more income on the streets than boys by selling their gendered and racialized identities. This is a complicated issue that has much to do with constructs of race, ethnicity, and gender. On the streets, young rosy-cheeked Indian girls dressed in colorful shawls provide a rewarding, though perhaps unsettling, folkloric experience for tourists. They are perceived through the lens of "imperialist nostalgia," and positioned as such, exoticized little girls can earn a decent income through begging. But the same rarely applies to indigenous boys. The vast majority have adopted Western clothing and now blend with Quito's urban street population. Unidentifiable as "real" folkloric Indians, they do not share the same exoticized appeal, thus hindering their ability to earn comparable income through begging. Rather, as boys they fit into the image of potentially dangerous street youth, perceived to pose a threat to the wallets of the middle and upper classes.

Regardless of gender, education has become increasingly important to Calhuasí's youth. In an open-ended survey question, 52 percent of youth between the ages of eleven and fourteen stated that they like to "study" more than any other activity. A further 88 percent declared that they would like to attend high school and/or university. As of 2004 there were six individuals from Calhuasí Grande enrolled in Quisapincha's high school and three individuals from Calhuasí Chico enrolled in Pasa's high school, a first for both of these communities. An additional fourteen individuals (including adults) were enrolled in seventh and eighth grades in a part-time high school in Ambato.[1] These young people will be among the first high school graduates in the community. Other children are keen to follow in their footsteps. With sheer determination on her face, twelve-year-old Monica told me, "I can go, I better go, and I will finish high school." These children and youth recognize education as key to the material wealth and signs of success they have seen in the outside world.

While many children express a desire for further education, it is difficult to tell at this point whether many of them will be able to achieve their goals. According to Calhuasí Grande's fifth- and sixth-grade teacher, "There are no good leaders who have finished school and followed on to high school in this community. There's no one about whom they can say 'Look at that guy—he was in school; now he's finished high school and he's really made something with his life.' Because this hasn't happened here, children believe, as some of them say, education isn't doing anything. It's useless. And there are others, others who are working, and they figure 'it's better if I can earn some money, buy myself a bicycle or something.'" Furthermore, many parents place little importance on formal education. The teacher continued, "There are a few parents who see education as important—we're talking about 1 percent here, out of everybody. But for the majority of parents, education doesn't really interest them much. If a child says, 'I want go to such and such place to work with other community members, with my friends,' the parents say, 'sure, even better'" (April 22, 2003).

An indigenous woman from the Proyecto de Desarrollo de los Pueblos Indígenas y Negros del Ecuador (Development Project for Indigenous and Afro-Ecuadorian Peoples) explained this way of thinking: "Basically, for indigenous people, they believe that if a child goes to school, he'll become lazy. Within their cultural belief system, they're right. Because when kids go to school, they start to spend their time playing, hanging out with their friends, or maybe going on trips. They start living by other cultural codes and changing the internal codes [of the community]" (August 28, 2003). Despite desires to continue with their education, children are often dissuaded from this path because of family and economic pressures. There is a conflict here between stated goals (more education, as expressed in their surveys) and the means to achieve it—a means that may conflict with their desire for the accumulation of material goods or, in some cases, for basic sustenance.

Perhaps one of the greatest problems for children is the cost of education. Despite children's universal right to free education as entrenched in the UN Convention on the Rights of the Child, education is not free in Ecuador. Rather, children are required to pay approximately thirty dollars per year to cover the costs of their uniform, school lunches, school supplies, and a "collaboration" for tuition. For large families, these costs are very high considering most cannot earn enough income from agriculture. Thus, to meet these costs, most children have to work. While some boys spend their weekends shoe shining in Ambato, most children leave the community whenever there is a holiday or a long weekend to earn money begging and/or selling gum. Summer holidays are crucial because in July and August children can earn the majority of their earnings for the school year. According to the director of Calhuasí Chico's school, some children are absent for more than a month at a time, especially around Christmas, which is a particularly profitable time to capitalize on Christian charity. In Calhuasí Grande's fifth- and sixth-grade class, some students missed more than fifty days of their school year while working on the streets, an absence rate that contributes to school failures.

All of these factors have been compounded by Ecuador's difficult political and economic conditions. The effects of the economic crisis, currency devaluation, and dollarization have been strong. Calhuaseños have been particularly affected by rapid inflation and rising costs for basic goods. Dollarization also meant that while women and children were previously begging for Ecuadorian sucres, they were now begging for U.S. dollars. This caused much confusion for Calhuasí's largely illiterate population. Furthermore, the nation's rising prices for basic goods and consumer commodities only reinforced Calhuaseños' acute understanding of their relative poverty. Thus, women and children have increasingly turned to rural-to-urban migration as a means to improve their circumstances.

Childhood, Gender, and Migration

Migration from Calhuasí is not a new phenomenon. Men had been migrating to work on coastal plantations since at least the 1960s. Women were left behind during these coastal migrations; they explained how during the 1980s the village was inhabited almost entirely by women, children, and the elderly as men sought work. The situation began to change in the 1990s, particularly after the construction of the road in 1992. Until then, access to and from the community was very difficult. The only footpath from Quisapincha ascends 2,600 feet (800 meters), winding its way up, down, and around several mountains. While the quality of the new road is poor (particularly when it rains), it has had a dramatic impact on the community.

The road was built largely because of the impetus of an agronomist from Care International. Tired of having limited access to the community, the agronomist helped mobilize the entire community into a massive *minga*, or community work project, to manually dig a route through the mountains. According to the agronomist, after the road was complete and the first car drove into to Calhuasí, the response was incredible. "They'd never seen a car in the community. It was amazing. . . . The emotion. [The community leader] cried. He had never imagined that his community would ever benefit from transportation" (May 29, 2003).

The benefits of the road were immediately obvious. Until 1992 the only way to transport heavy agricultural products to the market was on the backs of donkeys, mules, or in the worst case scenario, people. The new road allowed community members to hitch rides on passing trucks—although at first these were few and far between. The road also allowed better access to medical facilities, especially in emergency situations. Another significant benefit was the ease with which commercial goods could now be brought into the community. Coveted goods increasingly included cooking fuel, concrete blocks for construction, bags of cement, roof tiles, wooden furniture, bicycles, and televisions.

Significantly, another new benefit of the road was the ease with which individuals could now leave the community. Until the early 1990s out-migration was dominated by men. In approximately 1993 a small handful of women migrated to the city for the first time. These women were prompted to migrate after hearing of the successes of women in the neighboring parish of Pasa. Faced with deteriorating economic conditions, elderly and disabled indigenous individuals from Pasa began migrating with increasing frequency in the 1980s. Begging is a more or less socially acceptable activity for the elderly and disabled in Ecuador, since many believe that these individuals have few alternatives. As rumors of their earnings began to spread through the region, a few young women decided to join their ranks. According to an individual who worked with indigenous migrants at La Tola Shelter in Quito for thirty years, women's gradual involvement in begging was because "They discovered a modus operandi. . . . It began with a few people. But these people reported the notable advantages [of begging] back to their communities. Because the people you see here, they see a poor devil sitting over there and they just give. And I'd watch them when they arrived at the hostel. They'd get out their little bundles, they'd count their money, and they'd have a lot. So bit by bit, they started improving and started motivating women to come" (November 26, 2002).[2] Several of these women initially brought their young children with them because they were breastfeeding, had limited child-care options, or preferred to keep their children by their sides. But as they spent time on the streets, they quickly discovered that women with children could earn more money than women without. Henceforth, young children became integrally involved in rural-to-urban migration.

Between 1993 and 1996 the number of women and children involved in migration remained low. Those who did migrate frequented the streets of Guayaquil more than those of Quito. Although Guayaquil is farther away than Quito, men had already established a well-trodden migration route to the coast. Moreover, by the early 1990s men were decreasingly involved in plantation work; instead, many were working as shoe shiners and vendors in the city. By 1994 migration provided more than 80 percent of families' yearly income, the majority of which was earned by men (Rendon 1994). But by 1996, women and children's migration was gaining momentum. The acceleration of women and children's migration was attributable to several reasons, one of which was the Witches of Calhuasí incident of 1996.

Accused of taking advantage of indigenous belief systems for their own substantial economic profit, two white-mestiza sisters were captured in 1996 and held hostage in Calhuasí for eight days. Outraged community members demanded justice and threatened to burn the women alive, a severe penalty meted in some Andean indigenous communities.[3] In the end, the women's lives were spared because of negotiations with the local government; it was agreed that the women would be subject to an indigenous sentencing that included flagellation and a short prison sentence (*Diario Hoy* 1996a; Swanson 2008).

This was an event that garnered intense media attention to this previously isolated community. Media networks poured into the community to provide national coverage. An Ecuadorian television network won an international award and thirty thousand dollars for its short documentary titled *The Witches of Calhuasí* (*Diario Hoy* 1997b). The media sensationalized this incident, relying on racialized imaginative geographies of backward, barbaric, and savage Indians, who were threatening the lives of white-mestizas. In *The Witches of Calhuasí* documentary the network repeatedly showed the image of two blond, white women in their bras and underwear being whipped by Indians—thus suggesting both sexual and racial violence. According to an anthropologist from FLACSO, this video "was an absolute distortion of events" (August 20, 2003). In the words of the Confederación de Organizaciones Campesinas Indígenas de Quisapincha (Confederation of Indigenous Peasant Organizations in Quisapincha), despite the massive outpouring of attention focused on Calhuasí during this event, "nothing has changed. We remain out of sight and silenced in the Andean páramos, struggling against poverty, misery, and the injustices of this society" (COCIQ 1999, 7).

It is curious that many community members connect this event to women and children's increased migration. Few were able to provide a concrete explanation for this. It could be that this incident, which brought hundreds of outsiders—both indigenous and nonindigenous—into the community, revealed a different way of life to women and children in Calhuasí. It could be that this way of life prompted them to explore life in the city through rural-to-urban migration. It could also be because in 1996, after the witch incident, the Centro Ecuatoriano de Servicios Agrícolas (Ecuadorian Center for Agricultural Services) improved the road by building several concrete bridges. Previously, these parts of the road had to be crossed using logs, ropes, and the strength of many arms. Furthermore, by 1996 at least one community member had purchased a truck and was offering semiregular passenger and cargo services. This further improved women and children's ability to leave the community. Or perhaps the increased migration following 1996 may have been the cumulative result of the previous three years of intermittent migration. As word spread concerning the income that could be earned begging, it could be that more and more women and children joined the ranks.

The importance of the road's influence on rural-to-urban migration cannot be understated. According to an agronomist who works in the region, "After they opened the road . . . children would beg and cry for us to give them a ride in our truck, so that they go to the market and earn a few sucres [former Ecuadorian currency]" (May 28, 2003). Even young community members astutely observed the road as their link to the outside world and to cash income. Critical of the changes brought by the road, this agronomist likened it to the roads of the Amazon, which have wrought swaths of environmental and often cultural destruction along their paths. He said, "If there wasn't a road, the communities, well, they were really nice. They had water; they had culture; *they had everything.*" Perhaps in his mind, they had everything that an "authentic" Indian could possibly want. But at the same time this agronomist recognized the positive effects of the road, such as better communication and improved access to the outside world. He was conflicted in his desire to at once maintain the village in its perceived static and romanticized state and to recognize community members' very real needs. Nevertheless, he concluded by declaring that "Ecologists say that you should never build a road."

Men, women, and children's increasing migration has significantly impacted the community, particularly in terms of gender and sexuality. Migrants often return home with different attitudes toward gendered expectations. According to a Salesian priest who works in Quichua communities in rural Cotopaxi, "Men, husbands, and youth's migration has complicated rural women's lives. Because when the husband, the man, when he leaves for the city, he returns with different aspirations. He has a different view of women, a different view of sexuality, and when he returns, there are conflicts" (August 13, 2003). An indigenous man from the Otavalo region also spoke of how gender roles have changed in indigenous communities: "When I lived in Peguche, not that long ago, men and women both cooked, men did the laundry . . . there wasn't a distinction between his work and her work. Anyone could do any work, but now they've adopted more of an urban model" (August 1, 2003). In some indigenous communities, extramarital affairs, rape, and domestic abuse have become much more common (Sánchez-Parga 2002). According to a community member in her thirties, these things have also affected Calhuasí—particularly through youth attitudes: "Some youth return after having had relations with girls, without being in love, and they want to have babies. I don't agree with this. I didn't do this. I got married. I had someone I was in love with. He respected me. He loved me. But I say this because things are changing now. Now they grab them, rape them, and then they don't want to acknowledge them. This is changing everything. . . . We had a case where a son-in-law raped his mother-in-law. We can't have this. The children and youth that are leaving the community, they're different. They're not like before" (April 27, 2003). Through migration, constructions of gender and sexuality are shifting.

However, women are also gaining more autonomy in the community. Because women and girls can earn more than men and boys on the streets, they have become more involved in rural-to-urban migration than men. This is a reversal of the past wherein women were left behind. Now men are increasingly being left behind to care for remaining children, elderly relatives, and animals. As such, men are assuming greater responsibilities for laundry, cooking, and household chores. Although not quite a return to the "two-headed household," subtle transformations are occurring. Rather than the feminization of the countryside that Calhuasí witnessed in the 1980s, there is now a masculinization of the countryside.

Because of their experiences in the city and with various NGOs, women are also becoming more aware of their rights. Unfortunately, spousal abuse is highly prevalent in Calhuasí, yet women and the younger generations are becoming more vocal about their experiences of domestic abuse. Young women frequently asked me if my husband was "good," a question intended to gauge whether or not he was beating me. This question provided a way into conversations about spousal abuse. After I assured them that my husband was not beating me, I was able to inquire about their own situations, which often were not so good. While I have no evidence to suggest that women's awareness of their rights is improving the situation, I am hopeful that it will over time.

Women and younger community members are also reevaluating family sizes. Numerous teenage girls and boys confided that they do not wish to have more than two children. This is significant in a community where many women have given birth to more than twelve children. In fact, several are turning to birth control; in 2003 approximately twelve of the community's younger women were using IUDs.[4] According to one woman, "women aren't thinking the same way as they used to. Before they used to say that you had to have a dozen or half a dozen. . . . It's that, now, if we have a lot of children, we can't give them clothing, education, or enough food. So for this reason, women don't want to have many kids" (April 27, 2003).

Rural-to-urban migration is having both positive and negative effects on young people's gendered experiences. On the one hand, young women are gaining more autonomy and knowledge of their rights. On the other hand, urban gender ideologies are prompting some youth toward sexualized violence. The influences of migration on gendered divisions of labor are conflicting. While there is a fairly even gendered distribution of labor among children, these divisions become much starker among adults, as women are responsible for the bulk of domestic work. However, women's greater involvement in migration is reversing this trend because of the masculinization of the countryside. Women's greater involvement in migration means that men are having to take greater responsibility for household domestic chores.

Restructuring Indigenous Childhoods

Children's involvement in work, education, and migration is restructuring indigenous constructions and experiences of childhood. Thirty-five years ago there was no electricity, no running water, no education, no television, no road, no cars, and houses were made of mud and thatch. Since then, life has changed dramatically in Calhuasí. Western norms of childhood have infiltrated the community through education, television, and exposure to urban life. Young people are now acutely aware of a vision of youth that varies radically from their own experiences.

While some youth still marry young and most are still capable of heading a household at age ten, many recognize that their futures will not be agrarian.[5] Nevertheless, the majority (79 percent) of the children I interviewed told me that they would rather live in a rural community. But as access to land diminishes and as the land continues to erode, many youth are turning away from agriculture (see Pribilsky 2007). In fact, when the Fundación Don Bosco recently asked community youth from across Quisapincha Alto to compile a wish list for training courses, twenty-four expressed a desire for computer training and nineteen asked for musical training.[6] Only three expressed a desire for advanced agricultural training. The problem remains that there is no money to be made in agriculture. If youth could live in rural areas and earn income from agriculture, most would; however, at present their desire to live in rural areas conflicts with the reality that there are few means of earning income in the countryside.

During my survey I asked children what they would do if they won a million dollars. Reflecting consumerist desires, most said that they would buy a television, a good house, and a car. Some also added that they would buy a metal bed frame, a DVD player, or a sewing machine—all of which reflect the dire levels of poverty in the community. One thirteen-year-old boy in particular wrote, "I would build a twenty-floor concrete house and I would buy so much food and so many clothes, and I'd travel to the United States and come back after five years and buy a house on the coast." Informed by the materialistic lives of the soap opera stars that they watch nightly on television and perhaps touched by the "American dream," these children want a piece of that life. Very few children said that they would use their money for agricultural purposes. In total, 12 percent of children said they would use the money to buy animals, 7 percent said they would use it to buy land, and another 7 percent said they would use it to buy tractors. Although they have been raised as farmers, these children do not see their futures as agrarian. Calhuasí's youth increasingly want lifestyles as encountered in the city or as seen on television.

Many parents have high expectations for their children. Thirty-four-year-old Nadia wants her oldest son to be a lawyer. Her daughter, Nicola, wants to be either a police officer or a pop star. I asked a mother of a five-year-old gum vendor what she wants her son to be when he grows up. When she shrugged,

I asked if she wants him to be a gum vendor like her. "No," she said. "Something better." When I spoke to children outside of the classroom, their aspirations digressed from the seemingly sensible choices they divulged earlier, such as tailors, secretaries, and mechanics. While some still expressed desires to be teachers and police officers, others told me that they want to be "pop stars" or to "work with computers"—career choices clearly informed by the lives of the rich and famous.

Education is seen as vital to better and more prosperous futures. Children are struggling to graduate from primary and secondary school in the hopes that this will pull them out of their dire poverty. As of 2006 Calhuasí's road was graveled, which has increased access to the local high school. As a result, the numbers of young people pursuing their educational aspirations has risen substantially. However, a cautionary note should be added, because young people elsewhere have also pursued the same educational goals only to be sadly disappointed with their options as adults (see Jeffrey, Jeffery, and Jeffery 2008). For instance, young indigenous adults from rural parts of the Cotopaxi province have discovered that even with high school diplomas, many continue to work as migrant workers in the informal economy (Sánchez-Parga 2002). Katz describes a similar story in rural Sudan; fifteen years after her initial field research, she notes, "Education had proven no guarantee of anything" (2004, 195). Because of the existing social and racial hierarchies in Ecuador, it may be difficult for indigenous youth to obtain professional jobs after high school. However, the strength of the indigenous political movement and the Quichua education system may facilitate better options for youth from Calhuasí.

These ongoing changes are difficult for children. As illustrated by Pribilsky's (2001) research in southern Ecuador, a region heavily involved in transnational migration to the United States, changing child roles are a source of great trauma. As men migrate from these communities, children—primarily boys—are being affected by *nervios*. Pribilsky describes nervios as a commonly recognized folk illness generally attributed to parental neglect or abandonment. It begins with profound sadness and despair but soon transforms into open expressions of anger. If left unchecked, it leads to self-inflicted bodily harm and, in some cases, suicide. However, Pribilsky argues that nervios should be understood as a result of changing child roles produced by parents who increasingly seek to redefine their children within new ideals of modern childhood. He ascribes nervios to the breakdown of traditional forms of reciprocity and argues that nervios may have as much to do with increasing child-centeredness as it does with parental absence. He argues that the "mismatched placement of childhood roles and responsibilities is the greatest source of trauma for children in the rapidly changing communities of the Ecuadorian highlands." This has not yet happened in

Calhuasí, but children are increasingly struggling to find their paths. Poverty forces them to continue to work. To attend school, they must continue to work. If they want material goods, they must continue to work. Yet through education, the media, and interactions in the city, these children are being told that work is wrong. Rather, they are being told that they should be enjoying their childhoods through play, recreation, and study.

As a marginalized and racialized minority group, indigenous children in particular face unique challenges. As stated by the International Labor Organization, "The world's highest infant mortality rates, lowest income levels, most widespread illiteracy and slimmest access to health and social services are to be found among the world's 300 million indigenous people. . . . Wherever they may be, the 5,000 indigenous and tribal groups spread among some 70 countries around the globe tend to have one thing in common: they are the poorest of the poor" (ILO 2001). Negotiating these rapid socioeconomic and cultural changes is complicated for indigenous youth. They are being pulled in multiple directions and are unsure which path to follow. In the midst of vast intergenerational conflict, a process affecting indigenous communities around the world, indigenous children are struggling. At its extreme, this frustration is expressed through alcohol abuse, solvent abuse, and suicide rates that far exceed national averages—as evidenced in Aboriginal communities in Canada, Australia, and Brazil, to name a few (Survival 2004; Tester and McNicoll 2004). Unlike many other rural indigenous communities in the Andes, Calhuasí's engagement with the processes of capitalist modernization has really only just begun. Yet conditions are changing rapidly, which suggests the potential for youth crises in the years to come.

CHAPTER THREE

Migrant Childhoods

Street Work and Youth Identities

I'd rather be in my homeland (*en mi tierra*) but there's no work.
That's why we come here.

—Natalia, sixteen years old, Quito, July 4, 2006

When young Calhuaseños migrate to the city, they do so because they have few other options. Begging and selling are a means to improve their circumstances in the hopes of attaining more prosperous futures. However, in the city, conditions are difficult, as youth must contend with racism, social exclusion, and a reality that is vastly different from their previous experiences. Among urbanites, little is known about Calhuasí's young people; however, their brightly colored clothing and occupation of prime street space make the youth very visible in the city. Many myths circulate surrounding their lives, yet few organizations in the city have attempted to unravel these false truths. In this chapter, I discuss the broad context for street-working children in Ecuador and attempt to unravel some of the frequent misconceptions about working youth from Calhuasí.

As these young Calhuaseños migrate from rural to urban spaces, they must negotiate shifting and uncertain identity paths. Plunged into an urban and rapidly globalizing world, these young people are confronted with a diverse range of cultural, social, political, and economic forces that influence their understandings of themselves in both subtle and dramatic ways. In the city they must navigate through gendered and racialized readings of their bodies, which may not correspond to their understandings. Later in this chapter, I explore how Calhuasí's youth contend with these changes. I focus particularly on indigenous girls to explore shifting gendered constructions of ethnicity and reveal how youth internalize the racism they encounter on the streets. I argue that these girls are challenging, contesting, and redefining what it means to be an indigenous woman in the twenty-first century.

Street and Working Children in Ecuador

There is often much confusion surrounding what constitutes a "street child." A very small percentage of children who work on the streets actually sleep on the streets; most children return home at the end of the day (Aptekar and Abebe 1997; Hecht 1998; Kilbride, Suda, and Njeru 2000; Mufune 2000). In an attempt to clarify confusion and misunderstanding, UNICEF popularized the terms "children *in* the streets" and "children *of* the streets." The former is used to describe children who work on the streets but return to their families at night, whereas the latter is used to describe children who make the streets their home and have limited family contact. In practice, these definitions have been largely unsatisfactory because many children sleep at home *and* on the streets and maintain varied degrees of contact with their families (Glauser 1997; Panter-Brick 2002). Moreover, these simple categorizations exclude children who work on the streets *with* their families, such as young people from Calhuasí. The boundaries between street life and home life are fluid and dynamic, and these simplified distinctions are generally inadequate; they fail to account for the wide variety of experiences encountered by street and working children.

On the streets children are engaged in a multiplicity of activities, often moving from one activity to the next. In Quito children sell gum, shoe shine, sell flowers, guard cars, sell food, work in markets, beg, and perform. Estimates concerning the number of street and working children in Quito vary depending on the information source and the ways in which children are counted. For instance, a 1997 NGO survey suggests that there are 8,500 street and working children in Quito (*Diario Hoy* 1997a), whereas the municipality of Quito estimates that there are approximately 7,000. The municipality divides their figure into 5,500 daytime street workers, 1,000 temporary workers who migrate during holidays or agricultural downtime, and 500 children who work during the night (DMQ 2001).

Children and youth from Calhuasí fall into the municipality of Quito's category of temporary workers. The majority of Quito's temporary workers are from rural indigenous communities in the province of Cotopaxi, the parishes of Pasa and Quisapincha in Tungurahua, and rural indigenous communities in the province of Chimborazo (figure 2). These children usually work in Quito during the summer holidays, before Christmas, and throughout any other prolonged school closures (such as during teacher strikes). Children who no longer attend school tend to come during the agricultural off-season, which varies by region. The number of street children—youth who actually live and work on the streets—is unknown. Estimates vary widely and run between thirty and a thousand.[1]

Information concerning children who beg is sparse. According to a 1997 NGO survey, there are two hundred indigenous families who beg in the capital, an estimate I believe remains fairly accurate. The survey further states that six hundred children beg in Quito—although it does not specify whether or not these children belong to the aforementioned indigenous families. Based on my observations in Quito, I believe that approximately five hundred to six hundred indigenous children from Quisapincha and Pasa beg in the city; however, owing to the seasonal and temporary nature of rural-to-urban migration, these families work in the city on a rotating basis. During the Christmas season, this number becomes much higher, as indigenous children from across the rural sierra migrate to Quito. During the rest of the year, at any one time, there are no more than two hundred indigenous women and children in Quito—the majority of whom are from Calhuasí.

In Ecuador available data suggests that 40 percent of working children find employment on the streets: of working girls, 43 percent work on the streets; this compares with only 37 percent of working boys (SIISE 2003m).[2] A slightly higher proportion of girls may be on the streets because they tend to have fewer employment options than boys. Most work as domestic servants, vendors in urban markets, or informal street vendors. Boys, by contrast, have a wider range of employment choices and, aside from street work, are able to find employment as mechanics, trade apprentices, and workers on construction sites.

Based on national data collected by Ecuador's Defensa de Niñas y Niños Internacional (DNI-Ecuador; International Children's Defense Fund) and aggregated by the Sistema Integrado de Indicadores Sociales del Ecuador (SIISE; Integrated System for Social Indicators in Ecuador), it would seem that the majority of children who work on the streets are young. Between the ages of six and ten, 47 percent of working children find employment on the streets. Between the ages of eleven and thirteen, a further 53 percent of working children are on the streets (SIISE 2003m). National census data reveals that children begin working at an average age of ten (2003e). DNI-Ecuador data suggests that 39 percent of working children work four to six hours a day. A further 36 percent of children work seven to nine hours and 13 percent work more than ten hours a day (1997). Further census data reveals that, on average, children work five days a week (SIISE 20030).

In a DNI-Ecuador survey of 860 urban working children, 88 percent responded that they like working.[3] In my own research, I found that children often said that they liked working, but when they were pressed further, it generally became clear that what they actually liked was the money and not the work itself (which most found rather tedious). In the survey, children perceived traffic accidents and verbal abuse as their most significant risks. Among the young people that I spoke to, sore throats were another common complaint. These are caused by high levels of air contaminants and particulate matter in the city. Following the eruption of the volcano El Revantador in November 2002, the situation was especially dire in Quito because particulate levels were twenty-five times higher than acceptable norms (*El Comercio* 2002d). Medical research in Quito has further shown that children who attend school in the city's most contaminated sectors have four times the risk of respiratory infection and two and a half to five times the acceptable levels of carboxyhemoglobin (Fundación Natura 2000). Clearly these environmental concerns have a significant effect on working children who spend the vast majority of their time on polluted city streets. With the meager amount they earn, more than half of working children from the DNI-Ecuador survey said they spend the majority of their money on food (1997). Ecuadorian census data suggests that across Ecuador 52 percent of working children admit that they work to increase their families' income levels (SIISE 2003n).

Alison Vásconez and Fabricio Proaño (2002) have developed a typology of street and working children in Ecuador based on research in six urban and suburban areas: Quito, Guayaquil, Portoviejo, Loja, Santo Domingo, and Esmeraldas. This typology considers children's age of entry into the workforce, types of work, reasons for working, perceptions of work, socioeconomic conditions, and education. Their four categories include work that (1) provides skills and training; (2) gradually displaces school; (3) leads to "adultization"—early entry into the adult labor force; and (4) detaches children from childhood. This typology is important because it provides an overview of the nation's street population; however, much like the UNICEF categorization, it does not provide space for working children from Calhuasí. Working children from Calhuasí do not fit well into any of these categories.

According to the authors, children in category 1 (work that provides skills and training) are similar in many respects to nonworking youth. They continue to live at home with both parents. They work of their own initiative to garner work experience and to help their families with expenses. These youth begin working between the ages of thirteen and fifteen. They have completed primary school and most often attend night school to attain their high school diplomas. They work eight to eleven hours a day in stores, as domestic servants, and in trades. Their salary is much higher than most working children.

The authors believe that the majority of working children fall into category 2 (work that gradually replaces school). They describe this group as children who have not completed primary school but who continue to study. They often work only a few hours a day to minimize interference with their studies.

Nevertheless, many have been held back in school, struggle with their classes, and/or began school at a late age. Most abandon school after completing sixth grade. These youth live at home with their parents or stepparents. They begin working outside of the home between the ages of ten to twelve. For the most part, these children are boys who work as vendors and shoe shiners. The authors contend that girls from this group tend to work at home or as domestic servants. These children's earnings are an important source of family income.

According to the authors, a large number of children also fall into category 3 (work that leads to "adultization"—early entry into the adult labor force). The authors believe that the majority of these children have abandoned school to work, either temporarily or permanently. Most only have a few years of education and even though they may wish to finish primary school, they have not been able to do so. These children generally begin working at a very young age. In rural areas they begin working between the ages of five to seven and in the city between the ages of seven to eight. Their work activities are diverse and low-skilled, and may involve begging. These are often migrant children or children who live in suburban slums. They are usually from single-parent households headed by women. Their mothers are involved in low-skilled work and often have children from several partners. These children retain semiregular contact with their families. In most cases, poverty forces every member of the family to work, whether it be on the streets or in the home. They often spend eight to sixteen hours a day working on the streets and, according to the authors, are in danger of becoming street children. The typology suggests that these children have low expectations for their futures.

Like the children described in category 3, children in category 4 (work that detaches children from childhood) begin working at a very young age. However, the authors contend that in this group, children have completely abandoned school to meet daily needs. They are migrant children and are generally found in Ecuador's largest cities. They have only one parent and all members of their families either work or beg on the streets. Some of these children have abandoned their homes, especially in cases of elevated abuse. These children often spend long periods of time sleeping on the streets, if they are not already street children. Many suffer from nutritional and health problems and are often involved in drug use.

These four categories are designed to capture the vast majority of Ecuador's street and working children. Although they are broad enough to capture many, none adequately describe the characteristics of indigenous children from Calhuasí. While working children from Calhuasí are similar to children from categories 2 and 3, they are also quite different. To begin with, the vast majority of Calhuasí's children are not from single-parent families. Out of thirty-seven key informant interviews with Calhuasí's working children and youth, only one child had biological parents who were living separately; he lived with his mother and stepfather instead. An additional four children (two of whom were sisters) had fathers who had passed away. Their mothers had not remarried and, not incidentally, these children were among the poorest that I interviewed. The remaining thirty-two of the children that I interviewed were living with both their mothers and their fathers.

Rather than belonging to single-parent families, children from Calhuasí work on the streets *with* their extended families. They migrate to the city with their parents, their aunts, their sisters-in-law, their grandmothers, and/or their siblings. On the streets they work as part of tightly knit kinship groups. Through this extended economy of child care, children are most often under constant surveillance by one or more of their family members.[4] Their mothers, sisters, brothers, aunts, and grandmothers watch while they work on street corners or at intersections. Fathers and uncles, who work as shoe shiners, tend to move about in close proximity, thus extending the watch. Introduced to a world of non-Quichua speakers, busy traffic, and unfriendly pedestrians, children cling to familiar faces and places during their early visits to the city. As they become more comfortable and more familiar with the workings of city, social control is achieved through public teasing and ridicule. Those who do not conform to the accepted community norm are ostracized until they change their ways.

For instance, one night I encountered fifteen-year-old Tomás and twelve-year-old Carlos, who, inspired by Quito's traveling street performers, were in the midst of their first attempts at fire breathing on a busy street corner. With a small bottle of gasoline in one hand and a lighter in the other, they would take swigs of gasoline, ignite the lighter, and attempt to blow fire—all of which looked exceedingly dangerous. After harsh disapproval from their peers and family members (many of whom were working on the same corner), they had abandoned their attempts by the end of night. With particular persuasion, Carlos's older sister convinced them that they would "damage their brains" if they continued (September 13, 2003). During the early stages of this research, I also discovered that when I approached children on the streets, within seconds one or more of their extended family members would appear to monitor the situation. Because of the effectiveness of community social control and the high level of extended surveillance on the streets of Quito, the risks for children from Calhuasí remain low, particularly in terms of becoming homeless street children.

Moreover, children from Calhuasí begin working on the streets as soon as they are capable of doing so. They are often introduced to the city as babies strapped to the backs of their mothers, aunts, grandmothers, or siblings. When they become too heavy to carry but not yet old enough to work, mothers may

FIGURE 12. A mother and three of her children. While working, she carries her three-month-old baby on her back and her nine-year-old son carries her three-year-old daughter on his back. The three-year-old is just beginning to learn how to work.

place their children on the nearest corner with a begging cup or a box of gum on their laps. In these positions, these toddlers may sleep, play, or be entertained by one of their older peers. Occasionally, toddlers may earn some money from passersby but mothers do not really believe that their children are working at this stage. As they reach the age of three, children are capable of earning more significant income through begging. With the help of an older sibling or extended family member, they may bring in a few dollars per day. By accompanying and imitating their older peers and siblings, they learn to become successful street-level workers (figure 12).

While children from Calhuasí are generally poorly educated, many work in the city so that they can *continue* with their education. Out of those currently enrolled in school, almost 60 percent explicitly said that they work to pay for school supplies. Considering that the average family has five children, this is a significant financial burden for families. The children migrate during their two months of summer holidays, during their two weeks of Christmas holidays, and at any other given opportunity (such as teacher strikes or national holidays) to work on the streets for twelve hours a day. In fact, for the handful of students currently enrolled in high school, temporary rural-to-urban migration is the only way they can pay for their education. For these students work on the streets has become an enabling factor for further educational opportunities. In other words, street work allows children to continue with their education, the opposite of traditional thinking on child labor.

Working children from Calhuasí also differ from the categories described earlier because the majority are actually girls. While a greater proportion of Ecuador's working girls are on the streets, working boys outnumber working girls overall. National statistics reveal that in 1999 there were 26 percent more working boys than working girls between the ages of ten and seventeen (SIISE 2003f). Like elsewhere in the world, the overrepresentation of working boys has led to a greater research focus on boys than on girls (for exceptions elsewhere see Beazley 2002; Hansson 2003; Invernizzi 2003; Lucchini 1994; Rurevo and Bourdillon 2003). In most countries, the paucity of girls on the streets is attributed to a belief that girls incur greater risks—particularly in terms of sexual violence (Mufune 2000). Girls on the streets are also associated with sexual immorality (Invernizzi 2003) and are frequently stigmatized as sex workers (Lucchini 1994). Furthermore, girls are often expected to stay at home to engage in domestic reproductive activities (Kilbride, Suda, and Njeru 2000; Onta-Bhatta 1997). In Ecuador, young women on the streets disrupt mainstream norms and conventions because the social construction of gender dictates that women should be confined to the private sphere (Pitkin and Bedoya 1997). However, for indigenous girls this issue is more conflicting. On the one hand, indigenous girls are doubly oppressed because racist stereotypes dictate that they belong to the countryside and to manual labor (de la Torre 2000; Lawson 1999). On the other hand, Andean gender ideologies encourage girls to work in both the public and private spheres.

Perhaps counterintuitively, girls who work in the private sphere as domestic workers are often subjected to much greater levels of violence than they would on the streets. A recent study commissioned by the International Labor Organization in Ecuador uncovered that many young domestic servants—the majority of whom are indigenous—work under conditions comparable to slavery. Enclosed in live-in situations (referred to as *puertas adentro*, or closed-door, jobs because girls are rarely permitted to leave the premises), young domestics regularly suffer physical, psychological, and sexual abuse. In this particular study, most were rural indigenous girls who began working in white-mestizo households prior to the age of twelve. The majority of these girls earned fewer than thirty dollars per month while working nine to eleven hours per day, six to seven days a week (Castelnuovo y Asociados 2002). In an interview with the authors of this study, they recounted how violence against young indigenous girls is as much racial as it is sexual. In fact, if a pregnancy results, employers often consider this a benefit to the girl because her child will be whiter than she—thus *mejorando la raza*, or improving the race (December 12, 2002; see also Weismantel 2001, 154–159).

Young girls from Calhuasí are frequently offered employment washing clothes and/or housekeeping while on the streets, but the jobs are poorly paid. Even Viviana, an eleven-year-old girl, has received invitations to work in strangers' homes. Silvia, a sixteen-year-old girl, was offered a job as a live-in domestic at a salary of thirty dollars a month. Right now, she earns twenty dollars a week on the streets—money that she uses to pay for the costs of her education. Silvia is currently enrolled in a part-time high school in Ambato, which is very significant considering that there is not yet a single high school graduate from the community. Taking this job would have greatly interfered with her ability to attend school. Moreover, Silvia's home is in Calhuasí; she has no interest in moving to Quito permanently and confining herself within a stranger's home. Women and young girls are often offended when they are offered employment, especially if they are selling gum at the time. In their minds, they already have jobs as independent entrepreneurs—jobs that pay much better and are possibly much safer than those being offered. Yet their refusals of these employment offers only reinforce beliefs that they are "lazy Indians."

As a result, few—if any—girls from Calhuasí work as domestic servants. Instead, girls are encouraged to migrate to the streets, often before boys. In the rural Andes, girls contribute substantial income to their households—much more so than girls in the rest of Ecuador. According to national statistics, 42 percent of girls from the rural Andes contribute income to their families, as compared with a national average of 26 percent. Rural Andean girls also contribute slightly more than their male counterparts. Fewer than 41 percent of rural Andean boys contribute income to their families, which is almost equivalent to the national average of 42 percent (SIISE 2003l; see figure 13).

These discrepancies can partly be explained through differing gender ideologies, as summarized in table 3 from Antonella Invernizzi's (2003) research in Lima, Peru. Invernizzi delineates two types of families with street-working children: those with a rural Andean structure and those with a patriarchal ("machismo") urban structure (see also Miles 1994). Compared with that in an urban family structure, Invernizzi suggests, the gendered division of labor is less rigid in Andean families, as females contribute to both productive and reproductive labor. While females in an urban family structure may contribute the bulk of their labor to domestic-based chores, in an Andean family structure they work in both the public and private spheres. Contrary to urban families,

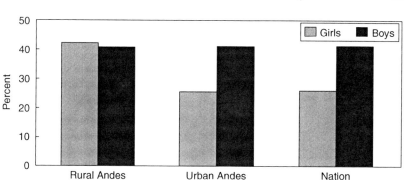

FIGURE 13. Percentage of children who contribute to household income.

Andean families perceive few, if any, negative moral implications for women and girls in the streets. Invernizzi's insights help explain the predominance of girls' involvement in street work in Andean Ecuador. However, these traditional gender norms are changing, as community members become informed by education, urban influences, and the media.

Life in the City

Compared with life in rural Tungurahua, life in Quito is dramatically different for Calhuasí's young people. Surrounded by concrete, fast cars, pedestrians, and pollution, children are overwhelmed when they first arrive in the city. Most told me that fear was a constant factor during their early visits. This fear stems from stories that they have all heard: stories about children who have been hit by cars, children who have become lost, and children who have been abducted. Although perhaps exaggerated at times, these fears are not entirely imagined. Last summer Agusto, a six-year-old boy from Calhuasí, was hit and injured by a taxi while chasing after his mother in the street. Shortly after this incident, his mother disclosed that Agusto was too afraid to come back to the city anymore. Nevertheless, perhaps out of necessity, within a few months he was begging on the streets once again. A few years prior to my fieldwork, an eight-month-old baby was abducted by a white-mestiza woman in Guayaquil. At the time, the baby was under the care of her aunt, who was tricked into passing the child to her abductor. Highly charged with racial meaning, this incident reevokes community members' fears of child theft. In these types of situations, indigenous parents often have little or no recourse—particularly since their young children are generally undocumented and unregistered.

Table 3 Working children's family structures

Theme	Urban family structure	Andean family structure
Work	Males are the primary income earners.	Work is a family affair and a moral duty for each member of the family.
Street space	Females are discouraged from working in the streets because of moral dangers.	Few negative moral implications for women and girls in the streets.
Gendered division of labor	Clear gendered division of public and private spheres. Males work in public spaces; females work in the home.	Gendered division of labor is less rigid. Females contribute to productive and reproductive activities.
Role of children	Children are discouraged from working and encouraged to study and play.	Children are encouraged to begin working from an early age, but play is an important part of work.

Source: Adapted from Invernizzi (2003, 324–325)

On a typical day, children begin working at seven in the morning. For the most part they work along Quito's two trolley lines. They occupy the narrow spaces surrounding the low concrete dividers that separate traffic from trolley buses. One step to the left or one step to the right at in inopportune time would have dire consequences (figure 14).

Every time the light turns red, youth upward of ten years old approach cars one by one and say, "*compre chicles*" (buy gum), with a few packets of gum lodged between their fingers. When they catch a potential customer's eye, some may give a supplicating gesture, while others may point to the babies on their backs and say, "*para el wawito*" (for the baby). Others may use different tactics and move rapidly down the row of cars until they find a willing customer. For young children the work is similar, yet most beg rather than sell. Children as young as three years old approach cars, extend their hands, and say, "*regálame*" (give me a gift).

From seven to seven, twelve hours a day, women and children spend their days breathing in exhaust fumes under the hot Quiteño sun, walking back and forth along lines of idling cars. At the end of the day, women and children working in the immediate vicinity gather together to take the trolley bus back to their rooms. Before retiring for the night, they purchase the following day's gum supply from a local convenience store. When I arrived in Ecuador in 2002,

FIGURE 14. Straddling the concrete divider that separates car traffic from trolley buses.

most of those selling relied on an Ecuadorian brand of gum balls. However, within a year, not only were there more individuals selling, but they had also begun to diversify with internationally renowned products of brands such as Trident, Clorets, and Halls. After purchasing their products at the end of the day, they then crowd into their small rented rooms wherein anywhere from two to ten individuals sleep on flattened cardboard mats on the floor.

As with many jobs, earnings vary from day to day. While one day they may earn $2.00, other days they may earn $10.00. Based on my interviews and informal conversations, on average women and children earn approximately $4.00–$5.00 per day. To attain this profit, they must sell at least four boxes or ninety-six packages of gum balls at ten cents a piece—which is a substantial task for some.[5] While this gives them a gross of $9.60, their profit is only $4.60. Out of this $4.60, they must also pay $2.00 per day in food, twenty-five cents per night for accommodation, and fifty cents per day in transportation. This leaves them with $1.85 profit. Because children under twelve pay half price for transportation, they can profit $2.10 a day for selling the same amount of gum. Therefore, if an adult or child works twelve hours a day, seven days a week for a month, they can return home with $50.00–$60.00 in profits. Compared with virtually nonexistent agricultural profits, this income is substantial. This income is also substantially higher than the income girls and young women could earn as domestic workers—one of their limited employment options within Ecuador's social and racial hierarchies (see de la Torre 2002b, 70–71).

These figures reveal why begging is appealing. Selling is difficult for young children because they are generally incapable of counting change. Begging also has no start-up costs and thus, other than room and board expenses, all earnings are theirs to keep. For example, a child who earns $5.00 a day begging can profit $2.90 per day and after a month return home with more than $80.00 in profits. The profit stakes in begging can also be substantially higher. Two occasional beggars admitted that young children can sometimes earn more than $20.00 per day. But to do this, they cannot be stationary at traffic lights—they have to be mobile. These children said the best place to work is in Gringopampa. Young children can earn the most, they said, because "they know how to pursue gringos" (September 10, 2003). In fact, few foreigners who have spent time in Quito's backpackers' district have escaped this pursuit. And because tourists often give fifty cents to a dollar to each child (compared with Ecuadorians' few cents to a dime), profits can indeed be substantial.

Nevertheless, few if any women and children willingly admit to begging. Even though they may reveal intimate knowledge of begging practices, they always conclude by stressing, "but I don't beg." Some admit that they used to beg but emphasize that this was in the past. When asked why she no longer begs, Juanita responded that "Begging is bad," suggesting that she has internalized some of the moralistic discourse promoted by local NGOs (April 30, 2003). According to social workers at the Fundación Don Bosco, begging robs indigenous women and children of their dignity. It also further reinforces negative stereotypes of Indians in the city. One of the former directors of La Tola Shelter said, "Work is dignity. . . . We tell them, 'If you hang around at the stoplights and cars give you things, if you put out your cup or your little pot and beg for a little bit of charity, [imitating them] "*papito bonito, patroncito bonito*," it's really shameful. But it's much more dignified if you get a box of gum or a box of chocolates and offer gum at ten cents or chocolates at fifteen cents. You're providing a service. You're working and earning your living in a dignified way'" (September 3, 2003). It is largely because of the Fundación Don Bosco and La Tola Shelter that many Calhuaseños have incorporated selling into their activities.

Many also dislike begging because of the harassment they receive on the streets. When I pressed Juanita further concerning her negative thoughts on begging she said, "Because sometimes people are rude to you. Sometimes they say, 'Why don't you work?' 'Why do you do this?' They say, 'Why don't you sell something? Then maybe we'd help you.'" She concluded that selling is better than begging because people leave you alone (April 30, 2003). Several others reported frequent verbal abuse on the streets. According to Malena, passersby say things such as, "Go get a job! Go wash clothes! Get off the streets!" (July 11, 2003). Roberto revealed that when he was younger, passersby told him to "Go tell your mother to get a job," an insult that would crush the spirits of many young people (September 10, 2003).

Selling gum does allow Calhuaseños to describe themselves foremost as street vendors. They resent being treated as "disguised beggars" when selling and insist that they are hard workers. But they may beg tactically when the opportunity arises. For instance, children often combine begging with selling; they may have a box of gum in one hand but the other hand outstretched. In this way, they can judge which approach is more likely to be successful depending on the passerby or attempt a different approach if the other fails. At the end of the day or on weekends, some children also engage in what they refer to as *yanga trabaju*. Depending on its context, the term *yanga* can mean humble, useless, in vain, simple, or worthless (Colloredo-Mansfeld 1999), while *trabaju* means work. If before the end of the day children have sold all of their gum, they may engage in begging or yanga trabaju until it is time to return their rooms. Or when they do not yet have enough money to buy a box or two of gum, they may beg to earn what they need. They do not perceive this as begging but simply as an additional or necessary activity required to supplement their income or as an activity to keep them earning until the end of the day. Thus when I encountered children or young women begging, they would almost always insist that they had "just run out of gum."

Another recently discovered way to make money is through performing cartwheels at traffic intersections, which can perhaps be interpreted as an ironic commentary on the image of the "child at play" (figure 15). When the light turns red, boys between the ages of three and twelve perform a series of cartwheels and then quickly go from car to car with their hands extended. "Cartwheel kids" surfaced on Quito's streets following dollarization. Most of these children are low-income boys from the outskirts of Quito or migrant boys from the coast. It is only recently that boys from Calhuasí have picked up on this trend. The trend was inspired by traveling street artists—youth from South America, whom most Ecuadorians refer to as "Los Hippies." These late-teen to twenty-something youth perform at traffic intersections as jugglers, fire breathers, tricycle riders, and acrobats and then approach cars asking for a collaboration for "Art in the Streets." Given rising levels of poverty postdollarization, Ecuador's street youth and street-working youth keenly noted the amount of money these

FIGURE 15. Cartwheel kids. The boy in the forefront is three years old, the boy on the left is eight, and the boy at the back is twelve. The five-year-old boy watching has a mother who will not allow him to do cartwheels because of the risks involved. When this photo was taken, she was working on the opposite corner. Also, note the two girls selling gum by the cars; the girl on the left is fourteen years old and the one on the right is eleven.

street artists were earning and began to emulate them—hence the cartwheel trend. Boys from Calhuasí declared that they could make three to five dollars per day doing cartwheels, and although tiring, it was preferable to selling gum because they could keep all of their profits.

Calhuasí's working children enjoy the money that they earn on the streets but do not necessarily enjoy the work itself. Roberto, who has been working on the streets since he was seven years old said, "Sometimes you get tired. Your feet hurt walking . . . all day, walking back and forth, back and forth" (September 10, 2003). Others complained about selling gum because, "We don't sell very much. . . . People don't buy gum." Consequently, "We don't want to come anymore," according to thirteen-year-old Nina (June 1, 2003). Those who beg also dislike their work because people criticize and chastise them on the streets. Others complained of the *solazo* (strong sun), headaches, and sore throats caused by excessive urban pollution.

While many of Calhuasí's children currently spend their earnings on school, others are saving money so that they can eventually enroll in high school. Fourteen-year-old Roberto, for instance, said he wants to go to high school but because his family has no money, he has to work until he can afford to. On the other hand, children from the poorest families, such as those without fathers, explained how they use their money to buy land, food, and animals. Although these children likely have the same material aspirations as other children from Calhuasí, their immediate circumstances are more pressing. As stated by Paúl, age twelve, "I just want to finish school as soon as possible so I can go work to support my mom" (May 5, 2003). Girls often spend their money on clothes, with new clothes being representative of status. For boys, the most coveted status symbol is a bicycle. While bicycles are somewhat functional in purpose, their utility is rather limited with the steepness of the community's Andean terrain. Therefore, for most boys, bicycles are purchased for status over function. Youth who have recently married or are likely to marry soon save their money to build a house. At age thirteen, Isabel spent the greater portion of a year working in the city of Guayaquil to save for her house.

The most sought-after houses are made of cement blocks and cement slab but these are expensive to build, particularly considering the cost of windows. Out of all the youth I spoke to, only Byron's family had one of these coveted *casas de losa*. Interestingly, his family had also previously owned a truck—a relative rarity in the community. Not surprisingly, Byron's family has been working in the city since 1993 and was one of the first families to become involved in rural-to-urban migration. Their first trip to Guayaquil was in 1993 (when Byron was four years old), and their first trip to Quito was in 1995. There are eight members of his family and their cumulative work has allowed them to accrue a greater number of material goods (such as a truck and a casa de losa) than the majority of community members.

Of the early migrants, most said they came to Quito for the first time in 1995. A former social worker at La Tola Shelter recalls first noticing the name "Calhuasí" on the registry in 1996, shortly after the Witches of Calhuasí incident. Their numbers continued to increase steadily after this point. In the year 1997 there were 126 Calhuaseño names on La Tola Shelter's registry (COCIQ 1999). These names belonged to men, women, and children, meaning that, at the time of this research, some Calhuaseños had already been working in Quito for at least eight years. Yet within academic and child advocacy circles, there seems to be much misunderstanding surrounding the lives of young people from Calhuasí. One of the reasons for this misunderstanding could be because that, with the exception of one small organization (the Fundación Don Bosco), no one works with this group of children.

Responses were vague when I asked some workers in Quito's prominent NGOs why they are not more involved with indigenous beggars. Many expressed a desire to incorporate these children into their outreach programs but were unable to express why they had not yet done so. Some suggested that there was little funding to work specifically with indigenous children. Others said that these children fall outside of their target group and for this reason have not yet been addressed. A provincial coordinator for the Programa del Muchacho Trabajador (PMT; Program for the Working Child) suggested that indigenous children do not want to participate in their street-outreach programs "because they're still caught up in their own cultural worlds" (June 30, 2003). There may also be a general reluctance to interfere with children from Calhuasí because they work on the streets with their families. Or perhaps because they work as beggars (a trade many do not consider to be "work"), they occupy a liminal space in-between working children and street children and are consequently overlooked. In Guayaquil, Calhuaseño children are even more neglected by social programs; not a single organization works with them. Most of the social workers that I spoke with had no idea that there were women and children from the province of Tungurahua on their streets. This oversight is not owing to a lack of visibility but rather to a lack of knowledge.

This lack of knowledge may be attributable to the disinformation spread by the women and children themselves. Calhuasí has traditionally been a very closed community and this position has carried over onto the streets. For good reason, Calhuaseños are mistrustful of strangers. They often lie about their names and origins, and feign miscomprehension of Spanish. Thus, they are partially complicit in spreading the myths that surround their lives. While these are coping mechanisms designed to push away unwanted attention, it is possible that their life circumstances could be improved if organizations better understood the varied factors pushing Calhuaseños into begging.

Urban Identities

In the city indigenous children who are deemed to be "caught up in their own cultural worlds" must navigate the difficult terrain that defines their gendered, racialized, and ethnic identities. Cultural identities have always been interactive and dynamic, and throughout history people have combined cultural elements to create new hybrid identities (Massey 1998). But as societies become more integrated in this period of rapid globalization, new fluid and dynamic landscapes are being introduced (Appadurai 1990) that transform cultures in both subtle and dramatic ways. But cultural globalization does not annihilate difference; rather, through relativization it encourages individuals to make sense of their life worlds by referencing not only embedded traditions but also outside influences and distant events. Local cultures absorb and articulate these influences in diverse ways (Featherstone 1990).

Dollarization symbolizes Ecuador's engagement with globalization perhaps most profoundly. The entire country now relies on the U.S. dollar as its basic unit of exchange. Individuals who will never set foot in the United States of America must use this dominant nation's currency to buy even a loaf of bread. New global cultural flows are also transforming Ecuador as the nation wrestles with its identity. Linking this process directly to dollarization, the director of PMT in Guayaquil had a particularly cynical view:

> This phenomenon that's happening, it's like everything happening too quickly, like we've been smacked. . . . We've changed our food habits; we've changed our family lifestyles; we've changed our clothing styles; we've changed our cultural tastes, all at an incredible velocity. I mean we haven't even finished understanding something, and just like that, we're changing again. This is transforming the appearance of our society in terms of what we want to build, [how we see] our children, our people. The poorest are involved in this dynamic too. They're not excluded from this. In my opinion, this is where the problem is. So [emulating a low-income woman], I have to find resources. I have to find money in any way that I can. If it means that I have to prostitute myself, then I prostitute myself. If I have to sell my children, I sell them. Anything I have to do to get money, I will, so I can buy myself some McDonald's. (June 30, 2003)

While perhaps an extreme view, her words illustrate just how profoundly people perceive Ecuador's engagement with globalization. In her opinion people are desperately scrambling so that they can participate in Western consumer culture.

A reorientation toward global tourism is also transforming Ecuador's urban landscapes. While international tourism has been part of Ecuador's economy for many years (particularly in the Galapagos Islands, for instance), in recent years the municipalities of both Quito and Guayaquil have initiated urban revitalization projects specifically aimed to attract global tourist dollars. The most symbolic outcome was Ecuador's successful bid to host the 2004 Miss Universe Pageant, an event viewed by millions around the world. Beggars in particular are perceived as a threat to these revitalization projects and, as discussed in chapter 6, efforts to remove them from the streets are ongoing. However, as urban revitalization attracts more international tourists to sanitized cityscapes, it also pulls beggars back to the streets. The global flow of tourism provides a substantial source of income for Calhuasí's young beggars; while Ecuadorians may give five cents to a child, tourists may give a dollar. For this reason, Calhuaseños work in the backpackers' district, in the international oil district, and, recently, outside of the international airport.

As Calhuasí's children become integrated into the urban sphere, they are introduced to varied outside influences that force them to question and renegotiate their identities. They traverse shifting identity paths that are both influenced and swayed by their elders, peers, teachers, the media, social workers, tourists, and indigenous leaders, among others. As stated by Blanca Muratorio concerning Quichua youth in the Amazon, how they "are going to incorporate modernity through the many neocolonial mirrors and at the same time reinvent their gendered indigenous identities is a crucial question facing many indigenous women (and men) in Latin America today" (1998, 417).

In Ecuador, clothing and language are two key markers of indigenous identity and their presence or absence signifies relative degrees of "Indianness" (de la Cadena 1995; Radcliffe 2000). Until ten years ago many of Calhuasí's men still wore white pants, red woven ponchos, and black or green porkpie hats. Women wore long, black woven skirts (*anakus*), red, green, or pink shawls, woven belts (*chumbis*), beaded necklaces, and porkpie hats (Chango 1993). While Calhuaseños' "traditional" clothing may be typical for their community, this clothing was once a symbol of domination on racialized and colonized bodies. Forcibly put on by Spanish conquerors, what is now known as traditional clothing is a modern variant of what was once used to distinguish and control Indians during the colonial era. Over time, these racialized distinctions were reinforced to draw sharp boundaries between white-mestizos and Indians (Lentz 1997; Radcliffe 2000).

As community members become more integrated into the urban sphere and outside cultural norms infiltrate community life through television, radio, and education, clothing styles are changing. Within indigenous communities, dropping traditional dress is imbued with meaning. As Sarah Radcliffe states, changing clothing implies "affiliation to the mestizo or national sphere, a 'putting on' of a non-indigenous identity, a disguise or mimicry of what it [means] to be 'Ecuadorian'" (2000, 175). The meaning behind this process is not the same for women as it is for men; the transformation of women into mestiza subjects is a much more ambiguous and threatening process (2000).

In Calhuasí, male migrants have imported changing cultural ideals in what, until recently, could be termed a "male mestizaje of the village." Owing to urban influences, young men now rarely wear indigenous clothing, whereas women have for the most part retained traditional dress. Language is also changing. Some male migrants prefer to speak Spanish rather than Quichua, but many women remain unable to speak Spanish with confidence. Indigenous men can manage to wear soccer jerseys, jeans, and Nike baseball caps without threatening their indigenous identity.

Despite young indigenous men's personal style choices, many express a strong dislike for Western clothing or cosmetics on indigenous women (Sánchez-Parga 2002). In the gendered politics of culture, women are often the grounds on which men inscribe ethnicity. In Calhuasí, the fact that women have retained both Quichua and traditional dress has subsequently defined them as being more Indian, which has further reinforced a perceived sexual and cultural inferiority. Based on research in rural Peru, Marisol de la Cadena argues that "indigenous women are the last link in the chain of social subordination: they are the least ethnically or socially mobile" (2000, 333). For the most part, women remain more deeply invested in the rural sphere and men are more integrated with the urban, allowing for the cultural mestizaje of the men but reinforcing the Indianization of women. Isolated from the urban sphere, women are perceived as unmodern and thus more stigmatized in the community's ethnic-racial hierarchy. Whereas men have the option of a fluid ethnic identity, moving between varied states of urban mestizo and rural Indian, women have remained at the bottom of the hierarchy of power and thus the most "Indian" of all (de la Cadena 1995).

As Calhuasí's women now join men in the cities, more and more young women are embracing fluid notions of ethnic identity. Isabel is a sixteen-year-old girl who has been begging and selling gum in Quito and Guayaquil since she was eight years old. At the time of this research, Isabel was entering ninth grade in Quisapincha's high school—making her one of six students to ever do so. Out of four boys and one other girl, Isabel achieved the highest grades. To cover her education costs, Isabel leaves for the city every chance she gets. Silvia is another sixteen-year-old who is studying part-time in one of Ambato's high schools. She has just completed seventh grade. Silvia works in Quito from Monday to Friday and then returns home for weekend classes in Ambato. Both of these girls are fluent in Spanish. Neither wants to marry until their twenties, nor have more than one child. While both retain elements of traditional dress, they are slowly incorporating baseball caps, T-shirts, and knee-length straight skirts (or "city skirts") into their wardrobes. Natalia is a sixteen-year-old who has never attended school. She married at age fifteen. She and her sixteen-year-old husband spend the majority of their time selling gum and shoe shining in the city. Natalia now wears pants—something unheard of just a few years ago. Indigenous girls who wear pants and baseball caps and who speak Spanish fluently are challenging their gendered, racialized, and ethnic identities.

FIGURE 16. Reformulating identities with baseball caps, city skirts, Cotopaxi skirts, and international brands.

Girls in the city also have more economic agency and are able to distance themselves from the label of "Indian" by demonstrating their affiliation to the modern through their consumption of consumer commodities. This development corresponds to Krista Van Vleet's findings concerning young female migrants in Bolivia. She describes how when girls return to their village for special occasions, they wear new, expensive clothes to "display their success, their ability to consume commodities, to attain a higher standard of living residing in a city with electricity, television, cement floors, and running water, to speak Spanish, and become more educated (or at least more cosmopolitan)" (2003, 355). As a result, community members have come to associate these adolescent girls more closely with commodities and the urban sphere than boys. As girls become more involved with the modern urban sphere, their relative degree of Indianness is perceived to change, which then partially inverts de la Cadena's (1995) notion—at least for adolescent girls—that "women are more Indian." Calhuaseñas' ability to buy city skirts, pants, and baseball hats identifies them as participants in a modern nation and the consumer economy. As girls become more involved with the modern urban sphere and more connected to Western consumer culture, they are challenging what it means to be an indigenous woman in the twenty-first century.

Yet while young indigenous women are now donning Western clothing, they are also appropriating indigenous clothing from other communities. They wear skirts from Cotopaxi, blouses from Chimborazo, and shawls from Otavalo. These are combined with Walt Disney T-shirts, Nike baseball caps, and sneakers—some of which are cast-off donations from urban residents. Their reasons for wearing these clothes in the city may be practical: skirts from Cotopaxi are cooler than anakus from Tungurahua. Young women are collecting varied cultural items and using them to reformulate their cultural identities (figure 16). As stated by Doreen Massey (1998), local youth cultures are "products of interaction": they are neither closed local cultures nor are they undifferentiated global cultures. Youth cultures are constantly reinvented as local, national, and international influences are accepted, incorporated, or rejected.

Nevertheless, many older community members are critical of these trends. According to Nadia, a thirty-four-year-old woman from Calhuasí, youth are changing the community's culture: "I will never take off my anaku. Even when I'm old, I will wear my anaku, my sombrero. But other women don't use these anymore. They sometimes go without sombreros; they wear city skirts. But not me. I always wear our culture. And our youth don't dress like they did before. They used to wear cloth pants and ponchos. They always wore ponchos; they liked ponchos, hats. But now, they don't do this anymore. They wear jackets [and] those big pants that are sometimes torn in the knees. Things are changing. They're not bringing good habits back to the community" (April 27, 2003). In and of itself, clothing does not constitute culture, yet clothing is a key marker of indigenous identity, as apparent in Nadia's statement "I always wear our culture."

Nadia is one of the community's key female leaders. She is a strong and determined woman who is struggling through seventh grade in an attempt to attain her high school diploma. But her declaration that she will never shed her anaku may be influenced by the indigenous political movement. Within this movement, traditional clothing that was once forcibly donned is being worn as an affirmation of indigenous culture (see Radcliffe 2000). But Calhuasí's youth are not catching on. Nadia's ten-year-old daughter refuses to wear a sombrero because she says she looks "ugly." She never wears an anaku. Instead she wears jogging pants under her city skirt.

As Calhuasí's young people become increasingly engaged with the urban sphere, they are also forced to negotiate their racialized identities through everyday encounters with racism. Perceived as "out of place" in the urban sphere through imaginative geographies that construct rural/urban racialized boundaries, indigenous youth begin to internalize these racist discourses that inscribe their "othered" bodies. For instance, on one particular occasion I was chatting informally with a nineteen-year-old woman and a thirteen-year-old girl, when they began to whisper and share embarrassed giggles among themselves. When I prompted them to include me in their murmurings, the nineteen-year-old asked me, "Do you have a cure for our faces?" "What for?" I inquired, suspecting she had some sort of skin problem. "To be more white," she replied. "Why?" I asked, startled by her response. "Because we're black. We need it" (July 28, 2003). The skin "problem" that these young women had was that they wanted me to "cure" their "black" faces. Seeing me as a white woman, they wondered if perhaps I had discovered a solution that could help them. This conversation reveals how youth have been indoctrinated by the glorification of white skin and a national discourse that suggests that to be white is to belong to the nation. It reveals how they have internalized racism and how this discourse deeply affects their understanding of themselves and their place in Ecuador's racialized hierarchy (see Miles 2000).

Racist discourses pervade Ecuador. Muratorio describes how Quichua grandmothers believe that they are losing the struggle for cultural reproduction in their indigenous communities. They perceive the invasion of televisions into their homes as unfair competition in relation to their own language of socialization because girls seek to imitate the images and lifestyles they witness on the screen. Muratorio states, "On national television indigenous peoples are represented primarily as a group in the news coverage of folkloric events and mass political rallies or protest marches. The large majority of the television images internalized by the young girls are racially coded to represent the aesthetic and social superiority of whiteness" (1998, 416). Elders fear that notions of culture, kinship, and sexuality are changing for the worse in light of a globalizing cultural economy.

According to a social worker from Guayaquil, "One of our biggest problems is that we have a weak national identity. . . . We don't want to be known as Indians, we don't want to be known as blacks, and we don't want to be known as mestizos. . . . More than anything, we all want to be white. We all want to have blue eyes and blond hair" (June 30, 2003). This is particularly the case for Ecuador's youth. A 1994 survey of youth between the ages of six and seventeen revealed that 26 percent of youth self-identify as white (SIISE 2003h). Among adults this figure drops to 10 percent, as evidenced by 2001 census data (2003b). While it is possible that these significant discrepancies could be partly explained by the seven-year time difference, I believe that they have as much to do with generational differences. When compared with existing demographic data, both of these figures are substantially elevated. The Consejo de Desarrollo de las Nacionalidades y Pueblos del Ecuador (CODENPE; Council for the Development of the Nationalities and Peoples of Ecuador), for instance, suggests that 1 percent of Ecuador's population is white. CODENPE further suggests that 30 to

Table 4 Ethnic-racial self-identification

Identification	Adults (2001)	Youth (1994)
Mestizo	77 percent	58 percent
White	10 percent	26 percent
Black	2.2 percent	7 percent
Mulatto	2.7 percent	—
Indigenous	6.8 percent	2 percent

Source: SIISE 2003f, 2003h

40 percent of the population is indigenous (Whitten 2003). Perhaps revealing a profound internalization of racism and the process of blanqueamiento, only 6.8 percent of adults and a mere 2 percent of youth choose to self-identify as indigenous (SIISE 2003h; see table 4). These figures suggest that youth internalize racism differently than adults. Perhaps more keen to fit into dominant imaginaries of the nation, youth more willingly discard their ethnic and racial identities.

Indigenous peoples across the Americas have long been engaged in a constant and often painful "process of self-modernization" (Platt 1992, 144; Muratorio 1998, 418). Since children and youth have become involved in rural-to-urban migration in 1993, this process has accelerated and distressed many community members, even those in their thirties: "Children and youth who leave the community are different. They're not like before" (April 27, 2003). This rapid intergenerational change is reshaping the fabric of the community, as Calhuasí's children and youth actively challenge, contest, and redefine what it means to be a twenty-first-century Indian.

CHAPTER FOUR

Antibegging Rhetoric

Gendered Beggars, Child Beggars, and "Disguised" Beggars

> They like the easy life. . . . They prefer to sit and beg.
> —Social worker, Quito, July 29, 2003

Life in the city is challenging for women and children from Calhuasí. Their difficulties are compounded by media portrayals and popular misconceptions that unfairly misrepresent their life circumstances. In this chapter I explore how rhetoric pertaining to indigenous beggars informs policy and practice to exclude indigenous women and children from the streets. I focus particularly on the rhetoric being produced and reproduced by urban planners, social workers, religious leaders, and the media. Within these groups, indigenous women and children are regularly described in terms of child exploitation and delinquency, false manipulation of public sympathies, ignorance, laziness, and filth. They are further described as being "out of place" in urban areas. I argue that these types of rhetoric draw attention away from problems associated with market economies that fail to redistribute wealth to the poor by instead focusing on the alleged vices of beggars themselves.

As a counterpoint to these rhetorics I also explore the ways in which indigenous women and children work with and around oppressive conditions and mobilize them to their own advantage. Cindi Katz suggests that the term *resistance* is often used too broadly to encompass a wide array of social practices that could be construed as oppositional. Instead, she distinguishes between *resilience*—autonomous initiatives that allow people to shore up their resources and get by each day; *reworking*—practices that attempt to recalibrate or rework oppressive and unequal circumstances; and *resistance*—methods intended to subvert or disrupt conditions of exploitation or oppression (2004, 242).

I find these distinctions useful when discussing the lives of indigenous beggars, particularly in terms of child "renting," a practice whereby the presence of children has become integral to women's begging tactics. Women and children have also begun to rework conditions in their village to overcome dire poverty. I discuss instances of reworking and resilience to suggest that indigenous women and children are not passive victims in the face of oppressive socioeconomic conditions; rather, they actively engage with and rework the forces that affect their everyday lives.

The Offensive Beggar

Before exploring how women and children contend with their representations in the city, I want to delve briefly into the academic literature on begging to uncover how begging has become negatively framed within moralistic rhetorics and criminalized through legal codes. Despite the prevalence of beggars throughout the world, there has been very little Anglo-American research on beggars beyond North America and northern Europe (exceptions include Chaudhuri 1987; Martínez Novo 2003; Schak 1988). Within North America and Britain, much of the contemporary research on begging explores the issue through the lens of homelessness and focuses particularly on men (e.g., Dean 1999; Duncan 1978; Fitzpatrick and Kennedy 2001; Lankenau 1999; Snow and Anderson 1993; Wardhaugh 1996). While valuable, this literature is not entirely relevant to the situation of women and children in Ecuador; however, it is helpful in unraveling how moralistic rhetoric based on the circumstances of homeless men in the Global North is being used to regulate beggars in Ecuador, despite a vastly different political, economic, and social landscape.

Historically, charitable donations to the poor have been indicative of personal goodness and regarded as the moral duty of upright citizens. Almsgiving has played an important role in poverty relief and has been widely advocated within most major religious traditions. However, as industrialized societies developed and social welfare systems evolved, the state came to replace the individual donor in redistributing wealth (Dean 1999). In fact, by the nineteenth century indiscriminate almsgivers were held responsible for the "demoralization" of the working class and targeted to control further outpouring of beggars (Stedman Jones 1971). According to Joe Hermer (forthcoming), this shift was emblematic of changing notions of charity and public space. In recent years these notions have manifested through diverted giving campaigns, which discourage individual gifts to beggars in favor of organized giving. In this way the organized charity replaces the indiscriminate giver to discern between the truly "deserving poor" and morally questionable "impostors." Donors are thus assured that their donations will be put to "good" use (Dean 1999).

Much of the criticism directed at beggars is imbued with discourse concerning the deserving versus the undeserving poor. In Britain this distinction arose in the 1600s and had much to do with a decline in monastic charity and an emerging emphasis on the belief that good Christians must work to pay their way. The deserving poor were constructed as widows, orphans, and the disabled. The undeserving were those who were able-bodied and thus capable of working (Hermer, forthcoming). In Ecuador similar types of discourse permeated early legal codes, although the distinction was framed in terms of the "solemn poor" versus the "wretched." Heavy emphasis was placed on the honorable character of the poor, judgment of which largely depended on the individual's race and gender (Milton 2005).

While giving has traditionally been equated with goodness, receiving has been understood as a moral failing (Erskine and McIntosh 1999). As stated by Marcel Mauss, "To give is to show one's superiority. . . . To accept without returning or repaying more is to face subordination, to become a client and subservient" (1966, 72). In the vast majority of societies, gift exchanges are understood as reciprocal transactions. The timescale and shape of this reciprocity may differ but ultimately gifting becomes a perpetual cycle of exchange where honor and status are at stake. Thus, in the words of Mary Douglas (1990), there is no such thing as a "free gift."

For the beggar, who takes but gives nothing in return, accepting charity with no thought of reciprocity or repayment inevitably implies a loss of honor. Perceived within the context of gift economies, the beggar is understood as lowly and inferior. In other words, charity is wounding for those who accept it (Mauss 1966). For the giver, however, charity implies an increase in status and honor. By donating cash and material goods in public spaces, givers gain public esteem by proving both their moral goodness and material solvency. Street-begging transactions are always publicly performed transactions. Regardless of what may be gained or lost, begging encounters are often highly disquieting moments that elicit a wide range of emotional and physical responses.

Begging is most often addressed under criminal law. In Ecuador begging in and of itself is not illegal. Rather, the law stresses the potential criminality and deceitful nature of beggars. Listed under the rubric of Public Safety, articles 383 to 385 dictate that beggars who carry false documents, feign sickness, or carry weapons or picklocks are liable to three months to one year in prison. A "disguised" beggar or a beggar who escapes from the authorities is liable to two months to one year in prison (Congreso Nacional 2003).

The penal code in Ecuador provides no definition of a disguised beggar, but over the last few centuries critics have written much about begging "impostors" (Murdoch 2003; Rose 1988). Beggars are often constructed as highly suspicious characters. They are described as frauds who fabricate wounds and forge illnesses or as clever professionals who rely on ruse and disguise. In the Victorian city, beggars were perceived as wealthy con artists who preyed on the generous hearts of hardworking souls. At the end of the day, it was said that they would shed their costumes to celebrate like kings (Rose 1988). At its core, this emphasis on the deceitful nature of beggars effectively works to question the credibility of their poverty. By suggesting that beggars are selling a false image of poverty, attention is drawn away from the inadequacies of market economies to emphasize instead the corruptibility of the poor themselves.

This is precisely what is happening with indigenous beggars in Ecuador. They are accused of not only manipulating public sympathies but also exploiting children and being ignorant and lazy. Child beggars are described alternatively in terms of innocence, corruptibility, or potential criminality. Both women and children are understood as being fundamentally out of place in the city. Very little emphasis is placed on the factors that drive indigenous women and children onto the streets.

Disguised Beggars, Gendered Beggars, and Child Beggars

While the vast majority of Calhuaseños began their street careers as beggars, in recent years they have been increasingly selling gum, mostly in response to pressure from a local NGO that has tried to persuade them that selling allows them to retain their dignity. The argument is that if they fit into normative definitions of work, they will earn more respect on the streets. Yet regardless of whether indigenous women beg or sell, many continue to perceive them as disguised beggars. One social worker explained, "If they try to provoke pity and people buy their product because of this pity, then they're begging" (June 30, 2003). The complaint is that they do not market their products per se but rather market their poverty. In the words of a municipal director, "It's that down deep, there's an intention to exploit the emotional side of the population. And so of course you feel more compassion when you see a little child only so big carrying her little sibling on her back and on top of this selling gum" (December 13, 2002). Or as put by another social worker, "They're exchanging misery for money" (December 9, 2002).

This raises the issue of how other informal street-sector activities are often categorically lumped in with begging. By expressing their very real need, indigenous gum vendors are perceived to manipulate givers' moral sympathies (and thus are understood as disguised beggars). Because the decision to purchase gum may be a moral decision rather than a commercial one, vending and begging are perceived as one and the same. Yet to convey need, at some level need must be performed; sympathy is inherently bound up with representation and theatricality (Jaffe 1990). Accusations that street vendors are disguised beggars who are "exchanging misery for money" relate to concerns pertaining to the presumed deceitful nature of beggars, a fear that these women and children could be selling false identities.

Rather than selling false identities, to some extent indigenous beggars are both selling and fulfilling their gendered and racialized roles as submissive Indians and as dependent women and children (Guerrero 1997; Oakley 1994). Supplicating for assistance on street corners conforms to popular imaginaries concerning indigenous women and children's subservience and docility. I found that Calhuasí's women and children are in no way naive; they are very aware of the need to perform these identities in response to gendered and racialized readings of their bodies (see Swanson 2005; Mahtani 2002). In this light, it could be argued that indigenous women and children's involvement with begging is actually congruent with the vagaries of capitalism; they are in some ways capitalizing on racialized and gendered expectations. In a very modern and entrepreneurial twist on resilience they are actually selling their racialized and gendered identities in exchange for U.S. dollars.

As a nation where machismo is well entrenched, able-bodied male beggars are rare in Ecuador. This contrasts to the situation in North America and northern Europe, where the majority of beggars are men.[1] Young Ecuadorian boys may beg but only as long as they appear young enough to do so. I have observed that as boys reach this threshold—somewhere between twelve and fourteen years of age—they may carry babies to help legitimize their acceptance on the streets (figure 17). Elderly and disabled beggars, however, are generally tolerated on the streets regardless of their gender. With very limited and inadequate social security benefits (which are fewer than eight dollars a month), many elderly and disabled individuals have no other means of earning income.[2] During an interview an urban planner expressed her willingness to help the elderly: "The elderly need to be protected. Many are kicked out of their homes and have nowhere to sleep. They have nothing to eat. So if I see an old person [begging], I do give them money" (September 8, 2003).

However, her view was very different for able-bodied indigenous beggars: "But if I see a strong woman, I don't give her anything. Because she has to, she can work. She can go look for work and bring her baby with her. She can find work doing laundry or housecleaning or doing something" (September 8, 2003). In her opinion, the "strong woman" is undeserving of her charity because she is able-bodied. She also believes that able-bodied beggars are simply lazy and "do not want to work" (September 2, 2003). Another municipal employee recounted her experiences with young women on the streets: "I've said to them, 'Come with me. You can wash clothes in my home.' And they've said no. So, [begging] suits them or it's more like it's easier for them to beg or sell gum" (July 25, 2003). Within these words, the emphasis is placed on capitalist

FIGURE 17. Thirteen-year-old boy selling gum while carrying his one-year-old niece.

productivity. Those who "do not want to work" offend this sensibility. Rather than being individuals worthy of compassion, they become individuals worthy of derision.

I found that able-bodied indigenous beggars are regularly described as lazy. According to a social worker who works with Quito's street and working children, "They like the easy life; they like everything for free because, you know, they'd rather be begging than working. Because you know they could get a job. Even young Indians—they'd rather extend their hands than work in a restaurant peeling potatoes or gardening or washing clothes. Rather, they prefer to sit and beg" (July 29, 2003). The opinions expressed by this social worker and the municipal employees reflect not only a view of Indians as lazy but also contemporary beliefs about the types of occupations indigenous men and women should occupy. In Ecuador, mainstream beliefs assert that indigenous women should occupy the highly gendered roles of washing clothes, cleaning homes, or peeling potatoes. Indigenous men should occupy equally gendered manual labor roles, an example of which is gardening. In Andean imaginaries, the indigenous body is assigned to the most humble of occupations (de la Torre 2002b).

Rhetorics surrounding sickness and hygiene also surfaced regularly, particularly during interviews with urban planners and religious leaders. A nun described begging as a "contagion" spreading through the Kisapincha communities (May 7, 2003). A priest urged the need to "eradicate begging so that there is no further *contamination* from this begging *sickness*" (September 2, 2003). The association of beggars with sickness and disease also resonates with popular imaginaries surrounding indigenous peoples; much like beggars are described as dirty, smelly, and diseased, so are Ecuador's Indians. This "hygienic racism" posits "a clean, healthy, 'normal' white population and a dirty, weaker, native population" (Colloredo-Mansfeld 1998, 188). Calhuasí's women and children are thus doubly stigmatized as "dirty beggars" and as "dirty Indians." Some city dwellers are repulsed by these women and children. Referring to an indigenous woman selling gum, an urban planner described her visceral response: "When it's a disheveled person, all dirty, I just have no desire to buy from her. Knowing that [the gum] in her hands, her dirty hands, all sweaty, in the sun [shiver of revulsion], no way! I mean, I just don't want to buy it" (September 8, 2003). While begging, women and children rely on begging cups—perhaps recognizing a general reluctance to place change directly into their hands.

Racialized imaginative geographies continue to circulate widely in Ecuador, where white-mestizos live in the cities and Indians live in the country (Radcliffe and Westwood 1996). Indigenous women and children on the city streets disrupt Ecuadorian norms and conventions; they are expected to remain in the countryside. Contemporary newspapers depict pictures of migrant indigenous women selling bundles of carrots and onions, while the articles describe them as being "out of control" and "invading the streets" (*El Comercio* 2002a). These types of portrayals repeat the colonial complicity in historically driving indigenous peoples out of urban centers and into the countryside. They present their re-"invasion" as deviant behavior that threatens to upset the imagined order and stability of the city.

In the Andes, as elsewhere, class, race, and ethnicity inform understandings of gender and public space. Unlike men, white-mestizo women rarely loiter in public spaces. As I discovered, women are subjected to sometimes threatening sexual harassment when alone in public. Married white-mestizo women who venture out without their husbands face much criticism and suspicion. Contrary to the majority of white-mestizo women, indigenous women routinely work in public spaces. Rural indigenous women spend much of their days working in fields, in public markets, or on the streets bargaining and selling. Nevertheless, within white-mestizo sexual ideologies, indigenous women remain out of place on the streets (see Invernizzi 2003; Weismantel 2001).

In Ecuador there is only one time of the year when able-bodied indigenous women and children are accepted in the city: Christmas. During the Christmas season pious Christians help "humble" Indians through "benevolent" charity. Recognizing the time limits of Christian charity, beginning in early December indigenous children line busy highways to supplicate on their knees. In the city of Quito the number of beggars multiplies substantially as indigenous women and children from across the Andes migrate to benefit from this ample charity. In the northern section of the city, brand new SUVs slow down to toss candies, clothes, and toys for indigenous children, who scramble onto the roads to collect their "new" goods. James Duncan describes these instances of acceptance as "temporal-spatial pockets of Christian natural law" (1978, 27). In a North American example, he points to the area immediately surrounding churches on Sunday mornings, when churchgoers "still got Jesus in them," as noted by one of his respondents.

For the rest of the year, indigenous children are no more welcome on the streets than their mothers. Children face competing representations through an emerging child rights discourse and through a more entrenched juvenile delinquency discourse. For the latter, the assumption is that, regardless of a child's situation, time spent on the streets will turn them into criminals. For instance, I attended a meeting between social workers, municipal planners, and religious leaders to discuss issues surrounding indigenous beggars. The position of these particular municipal planners was clear: street work fosters delinquency. According to an urban planner, children who beg or sell are "delinquents and drug addicts. You see children of three or four years old who are already sniffing glue. This is the future they have on the streets" (September 8, 2003). Or, as stated by a priest, "He may begin by selling candies but will end by selling cocaine" (September 2, 2003). To avoid this perceived inevitability, children must be kept off the streets through policies and practices designed to "save" children.

Low-income children and middle-class children interact with public spaces in highly differentiated ways. Middle-class children are kept off the streets owing to a heightened sense of "stranger danger," accentuated by vast inequalities between the rich and poor. While poor children work and play in public spaces, middle-class children are strictly confined to privatized and commercialized spaces that are inaccessible to the poor. Perhaps unwilling to mix with the lower classes, middle-class families deem public parks "too dangerous" even during the middle of the day. Simón, my eight-year-old, middle-class neighbor, rarely left his gated garden to interact with the outside world. If he did, it was within the confines and safety of his family's private car. His mother and grandmother constantly reminded me how dangerous the city was, evoking doubts as to whether these fears were real or imagined.

Contrast Simón's situation to Leo's, an eight-year-old indigenous beggar and street vendor. While Leo's family lives in Calhuasí, he spends the majority of his time in Quito to attend a school for working children in the mornings and to work on the streets in the afternoons. At times, his parents leave him in the city for fifteen days to one month at a time so that they can return home to tend to the fields. While Leo is left under the supervision of his extended family members, he is competent enough to get himself to school every day and work enough to cover his costs of living. By far, the bulk of his young life is spent working in public spaces, which allows him to attend a school where the quality of education is much better than in his community. Nevertheless, children like Leo who spend much of their time on the streets are stigmatized as criminals regardless of their situations.

Many view indigenous child beggars like Leo as products of "bad parenting." Yet these accusations fail to acknowledge the difficult life circumstances that push indigenous women and children into the streets. Leo's mother, Rita, is a forty-three-year-old woman with seven children, one of whom was a seven-month-old baby at the time of this research. Rita came to Quito for the first time in 1999 because her husband lost his job as a market porter. Along with her children, she begs and sells to earn money to support her family. Like most Calhuaseños, she works as part of a kinship group, and her children are closely watched by one or more of her extended family members. Rita wants the best for her children and is doing what she can. Yet for the most part women who beg with their children are perceived as women who exploit their innocent children and thus are unfit.

If women are constructed as unfit mothers, then "saving" these children becomes a legitimate goal. Mothers' exclusion in public space is thus framed as being in the best interests of their children. This further draws from a paternalistic understanding of Indians as innocent children who must be both represented and protected (Martínez Novo 2003). This view is often hedged in a belief that they are "bad mothers" because of their ignorance. The national director of a social organization for working children believes that these families "don't realize the dangers. I mean a family from the popular sectors doesn't realize that there are moral dangers. I believe they don't see them. If you point them out to them, that someone can grab their daughter, fondle her, abuse her, various things, many people don't see this type of risk. We as Westerners, as a structured people, perhaps we see these things more clearly. But they live in a world where this is normal" (December 9, 2002). Within this imagery of dangerous geographies, which relies on visions of villainous men lurking behind every corner waiting to grab children, there is a reluctance to admit that, statistically speaking, children face greater risks within the sanctified spaces of private homes (see Valentine 1996). This is particularly the case in Ecuador, where high levels of domestic abuse are well documented; estimates indicate that between 41 to 70 percent of Ecuadorian women have experienced gendered violence (Ponce Jarrín 2007; see also Pitkin and Bedoya, 1997). This is not to suggest that there are no risks on the streets; however, as discussed, the risks that these children face on the streets (particularly in the case of girls) might well be substantially lower than the risks that they would face as domestic workers, confined in the private spaces of white-mestizos' homes.

Another prevalent belief is that these women intend to exploit their children. A social worker for the municipality of Quito said, "We believe that there is a clear intention on the behalf of the family or of the adult . . . to use children to make money" (December 13, 2002). In fact, Calhuasí's indigenous women are often accused of "renting" children as props for begging—an accusation that fails to grapple with the complexities of indigenous economies of caring.

Child "Renting"

As previously noted, enhancing empathy is crucial to beggars' success. According to a social worker, "When people see a child in the streets, they immediately offer them money" (June 30, 2003). For this reason, in the face of dire socioeconomic conditions, babies and toddlers have indeed become important parts of indigenous women's begging tactics. However, the discovery that children enhance empathy is by no means unique to Calhuaseños. In China (Schak 1988), India (Chaudhuri 1987), Mexico (Martínez Novo 2003), Ireland (Gmelch 1979), and England (Hermer, forthcoming), women have been accused of renting or using children for the purposes of begging. Much like charitable aid organizations rely on the image of the wide-eyed, suffering child to solicit donations, it would seem that beggars throughout the world have long done the same.

When young or unmarried Calhuaseñas go to the city and do not yet have children of their own, they sometimes bring children belonging to their extended family members. In exchange, these women must return with 50 percent of the child's earnings and provide the child with a new set of clothing. From a Western capitalist perspective, this does seem like renting. As a result, during interviews social workers, urban planners, and religious leaders frequently criticized Calhuaseñas for renting children as props for begging. However, when I asked indigenous women for their interpretation of this issue, their perspective was quite different.

Rather than a purely capitalistic exchange, indigenous women perceive this practice as *prestando* or *mandando niños* (lending or sending children) a practice integrally connected to notions of redistribution, reciprocity, kinship, and skill building. By sending young children to the city with their relatives, indigenous women believe they are allowing children to get to know the city, which is considered a benefit for the child. There are key elements of socialization and training available in the city. Children who go at a young age learn how to earn an income and become more productive contributors to the family. Sending children is also tied to an economy of organized caring. It temporarily relieves parents of some of their child care responsibilities and allows them to focus on other activities. Furthermore, the added income earned by loaning children to sisters, aunts, or cousins brings in much needed financial assistance.

Child circulation is a long-standing practice among indigenous families (Leinaweaver 2008). According to a professor of Quichua and Andean philosophy, this practice has much to do with the redistribution of wealth: when he was growing up, his father, a weaver, was "loaned" several children in a sort of apprenticeship (July 25, 2003). When parents are unable to care for their children or if one of their extended family members needs assistance in the home, they may temporarily or permanently loan a child. The family member then assumes responsibility for the child's food, clothing, and shelter. In the city, loaned children are like apprentices and receive knowledge, food, and shelter. When they return to the village, a purchased outfit may symbolically represent that their clothing needs were equally met. Likewise, the shared earnings may be a reciprocal gesture to redistribute the recently acquired "wealth."

These types of child circulations and informal adoption practices are common in indigenous communities and serve to bind families together both socially and materially (Uzendoski 2005; Weismantel 1995). They are premised on the understanding that biology is not the only criterion for parenthood. Rather, in these indigenous communities, people become parents by feeding and caring for children over extended periods of time. It is the action and process of raising a child that creates parenthood. By building these social and material ties through child circulation and informal adoptions, indigenous peoples are better able to draw on these kinship bonds to cope with their social and economic marginalization.

When white-mestizo social workers, planners, and religious leaders criticize indigenous women for renting children, they are assuming the primacy of biological kinship and imposing a Western-based nuclear family structure. They are perceiving the exchange of money and clothing purely from a Western capitalist perspective, while this practice has more to do with reciprocity, kinship, and the redistribution of wealth—all of which remain important values in Ecuadorian indigenous societies (see Uzendoski 2005). This strategy also contributes to children's socialization and provides them with skills needed to survive on the economic margins. Given limited options within Ecuador's social and racial hierarchies, Calhuasí's indigenous women have learned how to maximize their families' earnings by incorporating children's labor on the streets. Rather than an act of resistance, this is a practice that reworks oppressive conditions in a way that takes advantage of social norms and Christian charity. It is an act of resilience that allows indigenous women to get by given few other options. When social workers, planners, and religious leaders point to women's "deviant" parental practices and argue that they are falsely manipulating the sympathy of the public by renting children, it becomes much easier to justify exclusionary policies and practices.

Reworking Conditions in the Village

For Calhuaseños, begging and gum vending have become key means to pull themselves out of poverty. Since the mid-1990s, women and children have cleverly carved out a niche for themselves, one that has allowed them to rework conditions in their village after centuries of state neglect and social discrimination. Although they remain very poor, their newly earned money has allowed them to improve their material conditions and better their educational opportunities.

Their path out of poverty has not been easy. On top of the harassment they receive on city streets, community members also face much criticism from their neighbors and other indigenous communities for choosing to capitalize on begging. Despite the lack of profitability in agriculture, Calhuaseños have been criticized for abandoning lands that could remain productive. Compared with other indigenous communities in the rural sierra, Calhuasí's lands are relatively fertile because they have not yet eroded to become hard-packed clays, as in the provinces of Chimborazo and Cotopaxi. And while the land is steeply sloped, water is abundant and the topsoil remains deep. Sister Diana, an indigenous nun who occasionally works in Calhuasí, espoused her views on the situation: "In comparison with other areas, this community should be very productive because it has lots of land and . . . the land is quite productive. . . . In other communities, they don't have as much land and individual properties are smaller, but they seem to be doing better. In this community, poverty levels are really high. Maybe it's because they've been left behind or maybe because they've chosen the easy life [*se han entragado al facilismo*]. Or maybe it's because they've had a lot of projects here and have become accustomed to handouts" (May 7, 2003). Other indigenous leaders are also critical and question Calhuaseños' motives for begging. Evoking the discourse surrounding the "deserving" versus the "undeserving" poor, a Pachakutik party leader said, "Sometimes people look for easy jobs, you know, they go for the easy life. So they abandon their little pieces of land—and to some point they're justified in doing this because it can take six or seven months for potato, barley, and fava bean crops to produce—but they come to the city to beg. And sometimes this is a bit contradictory because, of course there are [beggars] who have nothing, but there are also [beggars] who do have something but they leave their land behind and come to the city to ask for charity. . . . To me it appears a bit unfair because there are other communities that are extremely poor" (September 10, 2003). While not discrediting their poverty, these individuals believe that Calhuaseños could find other ways to get ahead. They also stressed that their involvement in begging further increases prejudice against Ecuador's indigenous peoples. According to Sister Diana, "It looks bad for indigenous communities because people believe that we're nothing more than beggars" (May 7, 2003).

Neighboring indigenous communities also criticize Calhuaseños. They accuse them of begging merely to build bigger houses and to buy trucks. This resonates with merchants' criticisms that Mixtec street vendors and beggars in Tijuana are on the streets "out of greed, not out of need" (Martínez Novo 2003, 257). The leader of one of Calhuasí's neighboring communities similarly asserts that Calhuaseños beg because they are greedy and lazy: "I mean they have land, they have animals, so those who beg build nice houses—nice two- or three-story houses." He claims that the only families that can afford trucks are beggars. He compares this with his own community, where no one begs and not a single family owns a car (May 28, 2003). Even within the community, nonbeggars criticize beggars. One woman complained that "with the money they make, they build nice houses, they dress well, [and] they buy land. I had to work taking care of animals to build this house. But other women, no—they build houses just like that. It's like being in town now because there are hardly any mud homes left. Now they build only cement-block houses" (April 27, 2003).

For some, migration has indeed become more than a survival strategy. Migration can also be an accumulation strategy driven by conspicuous consumption and status (Bebbington 2000; Colloredo-Mansfeld 1994). In recent years, *casas de losa* (houses made of cement blocks and covered in cement slab), trucks, bicycles, cell phones, and new clothes have become coveted status symbols in the community. Weddings, baptisms, and parties are also events wherein Calhuaseños spend vast quantities of money. On occasion, they spend an entire year's worth of earnings on a massive fiesta to elevate their status and esteem.

However, these parties also have much to do with notions of reciprocity and the redistribution of wealth, both very important values in Andean society. Traditional belief systems maintained that a lack of reciprocity within the community would result in personal illness. Throughout the colonial period, reciprocal gestures and redistribution practices were strengthened because these became crucial to basic survival. Modern examples of these continued practices of resilience are found in *mingas*, or communal work projects, where a rotating member of each family must share his or her labor on a weekly or biweekly basis through fiestas and ritualized exchanges of food and drink (see Weismantel 1988).[3] Through massive fiestas in particular wealth is symbolically

FIGURE 18. Boys and their new bikes. The structures behind them belong to the
Catholic Church (and are the nicest buildings in the community).

redistributed throughout the community, while ties of reciprocity are both created and maintained.

In recent years, many Calhuaseños are attempting to acquire a standard of
living as seen on television or as encountered in the city. In the evenings, families gather on wooden bed frames padded with straw to view Latin American
soap operas on small black and white televisions. Children understand little
but are nevertheless glued to the dramatic scenes as they unfold before their
eyes. They watch wealthy white men and blond women drive beautiful cars, live
in vast mansions, and work as high-powered executives—a world remarkably
different from their own. Through these soap operas they also observe a vision
of youth that varies radically from their own experiences and are led to believe
that they can obtain this (materially, at least) in the city. A Salesian priest explained how this process replicates itself: "When they see their peers go to the
city, they're jealous. They say, 'Hey, if I can buy a Walkman, a watch, sunglasses,
and a bike in the city, then let's go to the city and make some money!'" (September 3, 2003; figure 18).

While begging may have begun as a survival strategy it has since become an
activity that has allowed for both subtle and dramatic transformations in the

FIGURE 19. A new concrete block house. Note the lack of doors and the unfinished rooftop terrace.

community. That being said, I must stress that by no means are Calhuaseños now wealthy. While they may use their begging and vending earnings to build two- and three-story homes, the majority of these homes sit empty or partially finished while family members work in the city to pay off their debts. Most still have dirt floors and lack proper doors and windows. Very few are actually casas de losa because they lack the outer layer of cement slab. Rather, they are works in progress that slowly evolve as income becomes available (figure 19). These homes are also often barely furnished: furniture consists of one or two bed frames and perhaps a wooden cabinet. Most people sit on logs or cement bags to eat and, owing to lack of cutlery, must eat with their hands (figure 20). And while a few families now own trucks, usually the trucks are twenty to thirty years old and in very poor condition.

I refer to this consumption as "conspicuous" because, at the community level, these houses and trucks do reveal status. For instance, traditional homes were made of mud and thatch. Although damp and dark, they were very warm. The temperature was suitable for guinea pigs (raised for consumption) to live inside with families. But these new concrete block homes are very cold—particularly because most lack window panes and instead rely on loose plastic sheeting to

FIGURE 20. Inside the kitchen of a concrete block house. The family has a two-burner propane stove but prefers to cook with firewood because it keeps the kitchen warmer. Although the temperature hovers near thirty-two degrees Fahrenheit (zero degrees Celsius) at night, no homes have heating.

block the wind. They are, in fact, so cold that guinea pigs can no longer survive and must be housed in separate (and warmer) quarters. These houses are designed merely to replicate urban structures but are largely impractical for life at 11,150 feet (3,400 meters).

Although community members may use some of their earnings for conspicuous consumption and status enhancement, the community remains terribly impoverished. The "wealthiest" community members are often in serious debt from unpaid loans on their houses and trucks. While traditional homes can be made entirely of materials found within the community, the materials required to build new concrete block homes must be purchased. With interest rates at 18 percent, borrowers have much difficulty repaying their loans. As Sister Diana said, community members often tell her that "'we're going to beg because we don't have any money.' . . . Or sometimes they say, 'we have so many kids.' Some women have eight or nine children and they just don't have enough money to survive. So they go to the city" (May 7, 2003).

Individuals rely on migration "for ends that are more than merely ones of survival, and in many cases, have turned migration into strategies that both create economic resources and re-produce rural places" (Bebbington 2000, 510). Although begging began as a survival strategy, it now entangles conspicuous consumption and status. While there are many complex dynamics surrounding women and children's involvement in begging, their involvement has allowed them to rework conditions in their village and obtain previously impossible material and educational goals—such as a high school education, trucks, and concrete houses.

Begging to Get Ahead

In Ecuador begging is an activity that is allowing indigenous women and children to shore up their resources and move forward within the confines of a capitalist market economy and a racist social structure. Nevertheless, despite women and children's life circumstances, urban planners, social workers, religious leaders, and the media portray them as "lazy Indians." Children are accused of faking their poverty while women are vilified as "bad mothers." Because the lives of indigenous children are at odds with dominant understandings of how children should behave, their occupation of public space leads many to decry that their futures will be criminal. Yet these accusations merely serve to draw attention away from the flaws of the market economy, which polarize gaps between the rich and poor; instead, they focus on the alleged vices of the poor themselves. Constructing beggars as "lazy Indians," "delinquent children," and "bad mothers" then legitimizes efforts to push them from the streets.

Indigenous women are further criticized for abiding by models of parenting that deviate from the Western norm; however, these criticisms fail to grasp the complexities of indigenous economies of caring. Child circulation is a long-standing practice in Andean society, tied to notions of reciprocity, kinship, skill building, and the redistribution of wealth. When social workers, planners, and religious leaders criticize Calhuaseños for renting children, they assume the primacy of biological kinship and point to mothers' deviant parental practices. Here I suggest that Calhuaseños' approach to child circulation is a modern and resilient take on an age-old tradition.

Earnings on the streets have allowed indigenous women and children to rework conditions in their village and undermine some of the inequities in Ecuadorian society. High school educations are reformulating young people's agency and providing them with more options for their futures. Newly purchased trucks are being used to create new business opportunities, such as shuttling youth to the local high school. And new homes are providing impoverished community members with some of the status and dignity that they so desperately seek.

Far from being passive victims, indigenous women and children actively engage with and rework the forces that affect their everyday lives. Given highly oppressive economic conditions created by a prolonged colonial history of racism and social exclusion, begging itself can be understood as an act of resilience. It is an entrepreneurial way for indigenous women and children to capitalize on gendered and racialized readings of their bodies. Given few other options within Ecuador's social and racial hierarchies, begging is a strategy for obtaining their educational aspirations and improving their material conditions. The fact that begging is deemed a better option than available alternatives speaks to the continued oppression of indigenous peoples—an oppression that is both racialized and gendered.

CHAPTER FIVE

Race, Space, and the City

Whitening the Streets of Quito and Guayaquil

Quito Limpio: ¡Fuera mendigos, fuera vendedores! [Clean Quito: Out with the beggars, out with the vendors!]
—Social worker, Quito, September 2, 2003

On top of the harassment indigenous women and children receive on the streets, their livelihoods are increasingly under threat from punitive urban policies designed to cleanse the streets of undesirables. Under the guise of revitalization or renewal, cities around the world are reshaping urban spaces to revive city centers and attract global capital. While the language of renewal may seem celebratory, it is triumphant only for some. In a world where image is everything, the dark side of renewal is that it effectively erases or, rather, annihilates urban spaces for itinerant street vendors, beggars, street youth, and the homeless (Mitchell 1997). Neil Smith (1996) refers to this restructured urban geography as the "revanchist city." He describes the process as a vengeful, right-wing reaction against the poor by dominant classes that attempt to "tame the wild city" (16) and bring it under their control.

To date, much of the discussion concerning the revanchist city has been empirically grounded in the North (Atkinson 2003; Belina and Helms 2003; Hubbard 2004; Macleod 2002; Macleod and Ward 2002; Slater 2004; Smith 1996, 1998, 2001, 2002). In this chapter, I shift the discussion south to focus on the regulation of indigenous street vendors and beggars in Ecuador. I focus particularly on the cities of Quito and Guayaquil, which have taken their cue from the North to implement harsh neoliberal urban policies in the name of tourism. Relying on the imagery of cleansing (Clean Quito!) and modernity (Twenty-First-Century Guayaquil), these cities' urban regeneration projects are sanitizing the streets of urban undesirables, many of whom are of indigenous descent.

I explore tensions between the aesthetics of the city versus the aesthetics of the body to argue that the urban renewal discourse of cleanliness and modern progress is projected against the image of the perceived "backward," "rural," and "dirty" Indian. Keen to project a purified and sanitized image of the city, Ecuador's particular twist on revanchism is through its more transparent engagement with the project of blanqueamiento. Certainly, race plays a crucial role in neoliberal urbanism elsewhere (see, e.g., Fassin 2001; Terrio 2004; Uitermark and Duyvendak 2008); however, within the Ecuadorian context this engagement is much more blatant. In Ecuador's "modern" view of the nation, "dirty Indians" most certainly do not fit in.

In this chapter, I also explore how these concerns are projected onto the bodies of indigenous children. Critics decry the presence of indigenous children on the streets, arguing that the streets are no place for a child. Images of wide-eyed, suffering children are accompanied by articles that implore the need to remove them from the streets. A child's letter to the editor of *El Universo*, a newspaper in Guayaquil, reads, "When I travel comfortably in my air conditioned car it causes me great pain to see children the same age as me, twelve, who are suffering and humiliated, who risk their lives to beg from passing cars" (2003). While there are legitimate concerns about the well-being of children on the streets, it would seem that for some this discourse is more about the urban image and the incompatibility of filthy beggars and "suffering" children with tourism. This dialog further intersects with notions of citizenship and fears that these children will become the future leeches of society. Herein, I explore national-level efforts to remove begging children from urban streets, focusing particularly on a federal bill targeting indigent children and adolescents, a police roundup of Quito's begging children, and a proposed antibegging campaign. While these antibegging actions are put forth on the premise that begging destroys children's lives, I argue the opposite: that begging enables children to have opportunities that they never had before.

"Saving" Ecuador's Children: National-Level Politics of Exclusion

Ecuador's Code of Childhood and Adolescence lists begging as a form of child abuse, and many child advocates argue that begging is a violation of children's rights and exposes them to significant risks on the streets. Some of the commonly cited risks include deteriorating self-esteem and corresponding self-destructive behavior, health problems, traffic accidents, moral corruption, and physical, psychological, and sexual abuse. While I advocate for children's right to beg, I recognize that this activity is not risk free and is very morally fraught. Despite working within tightly knit kinship groups that exert high levels of social control (which limit the risks of abuse at the hands of strangers), traffic accidents remain a significant risk for Calhuasí's youth. During this research a six-year-old boy from Calhuasí was hit by a taxi on a busy street while chasing after his mother. His injuries were not severe but it was an incident that caused much concern for Calhuasí's parents. The reality is that rural children are unaccustomed to cars and have no conception of traffic speed. As a result of children's inexperience in the city, a Salesian priest joked that, "They throw themselves in the road like chickens" (November 26, 2002).

Several informants described the poor conditions endured by indigenous children on the streets. An employee from the Ministry of Social Welfare described an incident concerning a four-year-old indigenous girl: "She had a fever of 42°C [107°F]. She was lying on the sidewalk while her grandmother begged beside her. The child was just lying there, crying about her headache. . . . I remember we took her and we brought her to the hospital and found out that this little child [*criatura*] had bronchitis. If she hadn't received medication, she might have died" (June 3, 2003). Some stressed that young children are often inappropriately dressed for the weather and at risk of becoming ill. Others simply deplored conditions endured by these children. According to a municipal employee, "Sometimes, these children spend twelve hours a day sitting on the sidewalk, under the terrible sun of Quito, through the rain, through the cold, and these children just sit there. They sleep on the street; they wake up on the street. I mean, their lives become a little piece of sidewalk" (December 13, 2002). Clearly, conditions are difficult for children on the streets. However, rather than cite dire conditions of poverty as the driving factor pushing children into the streets, many instead blame indigenous parents' presumed ignorance. A Ministry of Social Welfare employee urged that "we need to warn them or educate them on the dangers of bringing their children, of the innocence that their children will lose when they bring them here, of all the risks they run—both in terms of physical and mental health" (June 3, 2003). So rather than focus on the larger structural forces pushing these children into these difficult circumstances, the causal factor becomes reengineered as bad parenting.

Conceptualizing children's lives on the streets in terms of lost innocence or as confined to a "little piece of sidewalk" has prompted some to suggest radical policies designed to remove children from the streets. While these policies are premised on the protection of children, I argue that they do little or nothing to actually help indigenous children but rather merely serve to remove them from increasingly sanitized city streets.

Protection for Indigent Children and Adolescents Bill

In 2003 Deputy Marco Proaño, a member of congress for almost twenty-five years, put forth a national-level bill titled "Protection for Indigent Children and Adolescents." The introduction to the bill expounds its motives: "There is a sad reality in this country wherein numerous children and teens are exploited, abused, and manipulated by their parents or caregivers. [They are] thrown into the streets to beg or survive under precarious and inhumane conditions, which affects their physical and psychological integrity, leading to malnutrition, disorientation, improper education, and general malaise."[1] In an interview Deputy Proaño told me that the state is obliged to help these children. In his mind, "Children's purpose in life is to smile. A child that doesn't smile is like a tree that doesn't flower. We need to defend the smiles of our country—our children" (September 8, 2003).

To protect these presumably unsmiling children, he proposed the following:

Children and adolescents who, by the will of their parents or caregivers, are left on the streets to beg or sell without permits will be removed by state authorities and isolated in specialized youth centers. The National Council on Childhood and Adolescence, the Ministry of Social Welfare and the chief of police will work together to design and execute plans and programs to remove indigent children and teens on the nation's streets. (Article 1)

Parents or caretakers will lose parental jurisdiction and all associated rights and responsibilities over their children. (Article 2)

All children and teens who flee from specialized youth centers will be apprehended and sanctioned. (Article 4)

This proposal sounds eerily familiar: it resonates with the former indigenous residential school system in Canada, the United States, and Australia, a system of forced removal of children from their families in the nineteenth and twentieth centuries. This punitive program was designed to assimilate indigenous children into white society and resocialize them as "proper" citizens. Much like the residential school system, Proaño's bill advocates removing children permanently from their families and placing them in specialized youth centers. Escape would not be an option for these children because the bill specifies that those who flee would be caught and punished.

The exploitation of children is a prominent issue within this bill. On a deeper level, this discourse intersects with the very notions of citizenship. According to Deputy Proaño, "We are turning these children into the future loafers [*ciudadanos fáciles*] [of society]. They're becoming accustomed to extending their hands when these hands should be used for working." He also believes that sometimes "necessity" is manufactured "to disguise laziness" (September 8, 2003). His words remind us of the presumption that because they are "lazy," Indians "prefer to sit and beg" and that they beg "out of greed, not out of need." The bill also reinforces the belief that children are on the streets owing to "bad parenting" rather than economic necessity.

According to a representative from UNICEF, Deputy Proaño's bill is "simply an aesthetic cover-up to hide children who beg and who defile the image of Quito" (August 22, 2003). The director of the Hospedería Campesina Don Bosco Chillogallo (Don Bosco Chillogallo Campesino Shelter) said, "He's only doing this for political reasons. . . . These are people who know nothing about child labor, nothing about social work. They speak their bullshit [*pendejadas*] and believe they're going to save us all" (September 3, 2003). In 2006 Deputy Proaño's bill was overturned because it violates the new Code of Childhood and Adolescence. In fact, it appears that Deputy Proaño failed to even read this code before writing the bill. The fact that a prominent member of congress with a long political history could circulate a bill that proposes to institutionalize child beggars in the year 2003 suggests that the child rights movement has yet to gain significant force. Dominant society still views children—especially street and working children—as juvenile delinquents with few rights.

Police Roundup of Begging Children

In 1999 the Dirección Nacional de Policía Especializada en Niños y Adolescentes (DINAPEN; National Police Force Specialized in Children and Adolescents) rounded up and seized more than fifty indigenous children in an attempt to deter children from begging in Quito. This plan came about through a joint meeting between DINAPEN and several of the city's child advocacy groups. According to a social worker from the Fundación Don Bosco, the plan was to first warn adult beggars that they were violating children's rights and could consequently lose their children. But in the social worker's opinion, DINAPEN performed a violent roundup of women and children *without* warning. The women were released the same day, but the children were detained in several of the city's shelters. According to the former women's director at La Tola Shelter, the mothers were terrified: "The women came back [to La Tola] all scared, saying that they had taken away their children and that they couldn't get them back" (November 22, 2002).

When women attempted to reclaim their children, authorities refused to return them to anyone but their biological parents. This proved problematic because many of the children were being cared for by extended family members at the time. The authorities demanded birth certificates but because many of Cal-huasí's children remain unregistered until it is required for school, few young children had these documents. Authorities eventually conceded that parents of unregistered children could bring male witnesses to verify their true identities. This meant that women had to return to Calhuasí—a return journey of eight to ten hours—to find the necessary documents or witnesses before they could return to Quito and seek the release of their children.

This event raises issues concerning indigenous economies of caring and contrasting constructions of childhood and parenting. The model of parenting imposed by the authorities in this instance stressed the primacy of biological kinship, yet indigenous children from Calhuasí belong to different economies of caring. Children are often cared for, for months and even years at a time, by members of their extended families. In Andean society, biology does not deter-mine parenthood. In the indigenous parish of Zumbagua, for example, Mary Weismantel (1995) described how "every adult seemed to have several kinds of parents and several kinds of children. They remembered a man who fathered them, but another who 'husbanded' their growth; they remembered a woman who gave birth to them, but others who fed them and taught them to speak and to know." Informal adoption between families, she says, "is an important tool used by families, households, and individuals to shape social identity: provid-ing each child not only with immediate care but also with the all-important dense web of kin needed to survive the vicissitudes of life on the economic periphery." Authorities imposed a nuclear family structure upon Calhuaseños and assumed that their deviance from this model was because of negligence, poor parenting, and child renting.

This situation caused much confusion and misunderstanding, especially be-cause many of Calhuasí's women have a poor comprehension of Spanish. Paúl was nine years old when his five-year-old sister was seized. She was in custody for over a week. He said that when his mother finally saw her daughter, "she put her hand in hers and saw her face-to-face and told her that she hadn't lost her mom." Paúl said that because of this experience his mother "won't go to the city. She's too scared" (May 5, 2003). For children, this incident was especially traumatic. According to the former director of La Tola, "The little ones, the ones that were still used to being carried around on their mothers' backs, cried and despaired" (November 26, 2002).

A major from DINAPEN said that "the idea wasn't to seize them aggres-sively but rather to encourage them to get into [the trucks] and invite them to our headquarters. . . . [This action was] perceived poorly by the public. They thought we were doing something unacceptable." She went on to say that their critics—largely in the media—accused DINAPEN of penalizing people for trying to put food on their plates. She responded, "We wanted to let [parents] know that they shouldn't make their children work because they face too many risks on the streets" (November 27, 2002).

Although critical of the police seizure and aware of the trauma this incident caused, one of La Tola's former social workers did see the benefits of the police seizure. She felt that overall, this incident "taught parents a lesson: you cannot use your children as props for begging." In her mind, "being poor is no excuse for being a beggar" (June 10, 2003). In the former director's mind, this police action occurred as a kind of threat so that indigenous women and children would go back to their communities "and to let them know that they *would* seize their children and that they *would* jail their mothers" (November 26, 2002). Nevertheless, within several months the majority of women and children had returned to the streets again.

Antibegging Campaign

In 2003 an antibegging campaign was being promoted by Anunziata Valdez, a former federal deputy for the province of Guayas. With support from the federal government, private enterprises, NGOs, and the municipalities of Quito, Guayaquil, and Cuenca, the campaign aimed to deter sidewalk donations to child beggars. The slogan *"Tu ayuda no me ayuda"* (Your help doesn't help me) suggested that almsgiving encourages child begging and aggravates children's personal circumstances. The graphics accompanying the campaign revealed a child beggar morphing into an elderly beggar, insinuating that once a beggar, always a beggar. In a proposed television commercial a young actor states, "As a child they told me that begging was work. People gave me money and I believed that I was working. When you're a child, you believe anything. Today I'm still sleeping on the streets and every night I dream about the same thing—not waking up. Giving money to a child might make you happy for today but it destroys a child's life." Rather than give to children, the campaign encouraged would-be donors to give to designated children's charities instead. The message was that if you give money to a child beggar you are in fact *destroying* that child's life. By giving to designated charities, donors can rest assured that their funds will be well spent.

Informants throughout this research expressed similar views concerning begging children: "If a child sells gum or begs . . . he'll obviously begin developing the attitude of a beggar in life. If a three-year-old child begins begging, by the time he's four, he probably won't want to study, he won't want to work—he won't want anything" (December 13, 2002). However, my research suggests the opposite: children do not want to be beggars for the rest of their lives, nor do mothers want their children to grow up to be beggars. Children and their mothers want the youth of Calhuasí to have a good education and to attain better positions in life.

In fact, my research suggests that their lives are not being *destroyed* by begging but rather that begging and gum sales are enabling possibilities that they have never had before. Children want to attend school, work, own big houses and new trucks, and live like those they have seen on television or in the city. At present, they have discovered that they can attain some of these possibilities through street vending and begging.

What is perhaps upsetting to these federal policy makers and child advocates is that on the streets, children's poverty is so visible and impossible to ignore. The purity and innocence of childhood appears defiled. But diverting handouts to charities or seizing and institutionalizing children does little to actually help their real economic needs. Rather, it merely covers up this racialized minority and attempts to push them back to the nostalgic countryside where young, rosy-cheeked Indians are deemed to belong.

Municipal-Level Responses: Guayaquil and Quito

At the municipal level, policies and practices targeting indigenous women and children on the streets are less than inclusionary. Quito and Guayaquil have been working hard to reshape their urban images. Like cities elsewhere, they have seized upon tourism as a possible remedy for many of their economic woes. As Ecuador's largest cities and the main gateways to the Galapagos Islands (where large-scale tourism began in the 1970s), Quito and Guayaquil are particularly well situated to benefit from tourism. The most symbolic outcome of this recent economic shift was Ecuador's successful bid to host the Miss Universe Pageant in 2004, much of which highlighted these cities' regenerated areas.

This new tourist-friendly image is of a city without informal street workers. While street vendors have been part of Ecuadorian cityscapes for centuries (Gauderman 2003), they are increasingly perceived as threats to urban revitalization and international tourism (Middleton 2003). Global cities like New York and Miami (cities that are imagined as lacking chaotic urban informal sectors) are the urban ideal in Ecuador. In regenerated sectors of Guayaquil, it is not uncommon to hear people praise the new boardwalk as being "just like Miami," a compliment of the highest order (Garcés 2004). Indigenous street vendors, however, do not fit into the global city ideal. They are perceived to betray Quito and Guayaquil's lack of modernity and backwardness to tourists. Consequently, efforts to remove them from sanitized urban spaces have been ongoing.

In the city of Guayaquil, U.S.-style revanchist policies have been implemented with particular rigor. Taking their cue from New York City, in 2002 the municipality of Guayaquil contracted the city's former police commissioner William Bratton to help overhaul the city's urban regeneration strategy (*El Universo* 2004a, 2004b). William Bratton was a key architect behind Mayor Rudolph Giuliani's zero tolerance policies, which were designed to clean up New York City. Key targets of these punitive policies included squeegee kids, the homeless, street youth and all those perceived as unsightly blemishes on the streets. These policies took inspiration from James Wilson and George Kelling's (1982) controversial Broken Windows theory, which suggests that intensive policing of low-level, antisocial behavior leads to an overall reduction in crime. This theory has since been widely critiqued (Bowling 1999; Harcourt 2001; Mitchell 2003; Smith 1998), yet it remains highly touted as a key municipal crime-reduction strategy. Drawing from his experience in New York City, Bratton suggested a high-tech anticrime strategy for Guayaquil, which later came to be known colloquially as Plan Bratton (*El Universo* 2002).

This new anticrime structure is part and parcel of Guayaquil's urban regeneration project, which embraces modernity in its title Twenty-First-Century Guayaquil. In this modern Guayaquil, urban undesirables caught working in regenerated areas face harsh sanctions. Beggars and itinerant vendors can be imprisoned for up to seven days, while fines can be as high as five hundred dollars. The magnificent and newly constructed boardwalk—Guayaquil's showcase for its affiliation with the modern and hence dubbed Malecón 2000—is monitored by heavily armed police, who individually decide who can enter the gated grounds and who cannot. Within the regenerated area there are now at least fifty-two police-operated video cameras running twenty-four hours a day. This municipal gaze is concerned not only with crime control; rather, a key function of the cameras is to monitor the regenerated areas for the occupation of public space—particularly by informal workers (*El Universo* 2003).

In Quito similar processes are taking place. However, the pace of this change has been slower and the regulation less harsh because of more left-of-center political leanings in the sierra. The historical center, which showcases Quito's colonial past, has undergone the most dramatic change in recent years. Although it was declared a UNESCO world heritage site in 1978 (Bromley and Jones 1995), tourism did not come onto the development agenda until 1994. Within this agenda, informal street workers were highlighted as a problem for tourism and thus their removal from the historical center was deemed crucial (Middleton 2003).

As elsewhere in Latin America, Quito's modernization discourse tends to conflate cleanliness and hygiene with progress. Spaces of modernity must remain clean (see Tomic, Trumper, and Hidalgo Dattwyler 2006), yet there also remains a colonial logic that perceives indigenous peoples as dirty and contaminated. Consequently, indigenous street vendors are blamed as the principle cause for a host of morally suspect and unsightly problems, including litter and public hygiene concerns. Of course, these problems could be overcome with improved garbage collection services and public sanitation facilities. But rather than focus on costly municipal solutions, it would seem that the municipality would rather sweep informal workers off the streets. Perhaps the problem is not the litter per se but rather the perceived visual contamination caused by indigenous bodies.

However, it was not until 2003 that the majority of the historical center's informal street workers were successfully removed, after almost of a decade of negotiation and deliberation (Middleton 2003). By May 2003 the municipality succeeded in removing 6,900 informal workers from the streets of the city's historical center. The majority were relocated to ten municipally run urban markets—most of which were far removed from the city center and, consequently, the tourist's gaze. By June the streets of the historical center were virtually free of informal vendors, largely owing to the presence of heavily armed police charged to monitor and regulate the area. The physical presence of the police was also accompanied by a new high-tech video surveillance system dubbed Eyes of the Eagle. While those who belonged to informal trade associations managed to relocate into these municipally run markets, those who were not (i.e., itinerant street vendors) were largely displaced.

Despite the glorification of U.S. urban ideals, it is curious that Ecuador should turn to the North for inspiration, considering its vastly different socioeconomic and political landscape. As Smith astutely notes, one of the dangers of the New York model is exactly that it could become a "template for a global, postliberal revanchism that may exact revenge against different social groups in different places, doing so with differing intensities and taking quite different forms" (2001, 73). This is precisely the concern in Ecuador, a country traversed by deep racial inequalities—particularly for indigenous peoples. Detailed empirical studies on the intersections between race, ethnicity, and urban restructuring are limited (see Taylor 2002; Wilson and Grammenos 2005; Wyly and Hammel 2004). Following Phil Hubbard (2004, 666), who states that he wants to pry open "debates on the neoliberal city by highlighting the gendered injustices wrought by neoliberal policy," I wish to highlight the *racial* injustices wrought by neoliberal policy. In Ecuador, the importation of revanchist urbanism only compounds already deep racial inequalities endured by the nation's indigenous peoples, many of whom make their livings in the urban informal sector.

Researchers elsewhere have also pointed to the locally distinctive strands of revanchism in the North (Atkinson 2003; Macleod 2002; Slater 2004). In

Ecuador revanchism is taking a distinctive form, largely by building on a colonial and eugenicist logic. On this historical foundation, it has placed its own neoliberal twist: a high-tech, police-enforced whitening of the city. Although indigenous peoples have long been part of urban cityscapes, city officials have decided to take the city back to fabricate a vision of the city in which Indians do not belong. This type of revanchism is enforced not only by underpaid, uneducated municipal police officers but also by private security guards, many of whom are too underqualified to become officers themselves, yet tote even bigger guns.

Revanchism in Ecuador is also being driven by a different set of criteria than in the North. Unlike in many cities in North America and Europe, beggars, street children, and informal workers are not being displaced to build luxury condominiums for the middle and upper classes; rather, they are removed to make way for the global tourist class. In other words, revanchism is not being driven by the demand for gentrified housing but rather by a reorientation of the city to the tourist economy. Tourism is often a justification for urban regeneration; however, it is generally only part and parcel of the process rather than the raison d'être.

There are also some contradictions in Ecuador's version of revanchism, as researchers have uncovered in cities elsewhere (DeVerteuil 2006; Macleod 2002). In Quito for instance the municipal police lack the resources to fully enforce municipal ordinances. For this reason officers must sometimes turn a blind eye to beggars and vendors in the streets. The municipality also supports social programs that, ironically, directly contradict efforts to cleanse the streets. For instance, the Patronato San José (PSJ; San José Foundation) is a municipally funded program that supports street and working children in the historical center. While the PSJ advocates for these children, officers forcibly evict them from the city center's sanitized plazas.

Sanitized Spaces of Exclusion in Quito and Guayaquil

While the quote at the beginning of this chapter (Clean Quito: Out with the beggars, out with the vendors!) is a sarcastic mockery of the Clean Quito! municipal campaign, it effectively captures some of the tensions between the aesthetics of the city and the aesthetics of the informal street worker's body. Indeed, the project of urban renewal is absolutely informed by a discourse of purity and defilement. According to one municipal urban planner, "We need to change the image of the city. . . . We need to fight to make this a better city, so that the city looks better, so that are no longer beggars in the streets" (September 8, 2003). In the city's newspapers, critics cite long lists of urban undesirables, including "supplicating shoe shine kids, ragged beggars with extended hands, migrants hanging on to threads of hope," who "degrade the [city's] beauty," who are "incompatible with tourism," and who are "the shame of the city" (*El Comercio* 2002b). Beauty queen candidates for the municipality of Quito in 2003 campaigned on a collective desire to improve the image of the city. According to one candidate, "As Quiteños we must fight the problems that tarnish the beauty of our city." Another made an emotional appeal and expressed her wish for "begging to disappear from all of the city's streets" (2002c).

As Tim Cresswell (1996) has described, particular places are often connected with particular meanings to strengthen ideological positions. Despite a long history of indigenous vendors working on the streets of Quito and Guayaquil, Ecuador's geographic imaginaries dictate that Indians belong in the rural sphere. Through hygienic racism, their presence in the urban sphere is constructed as a potential source of contamination for white-mestizos. This racism manifests itself in everyday occurrences: I was once with a mixed group of white-mestizos and indigenous peoples, when a white-mestiza doctor began to scratch her leg and complain loudly about being bitten by fleas, while looking around and noting that it had "been a long time" since she had spent time with Indians. To keep city spaces sanitized, dominant groups rely on strategies of social and spatial distancing to keep these defiled peoples out (Sibley 1995).

In Ecuador indigenous beggars and street vendors are perceived to threaten the "proper" meaning of urban space or, rather, the dominant ideological construction of space. If the ideological construction of urban space is to be a space of beauty or a space for tourism, then "ragged" beggars become incompatible with this meaning. These taken-for-granted aspects of place are used to turn attention away from social problems and reframe the issue in terms of the quality of a particular place. The issue thus becomes more about removing indigenous street vendors and beggars from the streets (framed in the common sense discourse that "the streets are no place for a child," for instance) than about trying to alleviate the larger forces that push them there in the first place.

My interviews with urban planners, municipal employees, and police officers revealed how these processes take shape through everyday geographies of racism and social exclusion. For instance, shortly after the successful removal of informal workers from the historical center, I interviewed Quito's chief of police to gauge his thoughts on what had happened. He expressed much admiration for the municipality's work: "It feels like the colonial part of the city again and I think it'll bring tourism, which is the principal object of this project: a source of income for the country and the city. In my opinion, this is a great accomplishment. But we need to maintain it and at the moment, it's my job to keep it clean" (August 5, 2003). By keeping the historical center "clean," the chief of police recognizes his role in preventing the perceived source of pollution—poor informal workers—from recontaminating the area. As a result, police presence in the historical center is overwhelming. Police pickup trucks routinely circulate in the area, carrying officers in the back who are ready to jump out at a moment's notice. Meanwhile, officers on foot monitor the area with large rottweilers in tow.

The image of the city is at the heart of these exclusionary strategies. When police officers were asked why they are forcing shoe shiners, vendors, and beggars out of the historical center's plazas, they replied, "Because they look bad for tourists" and "they damage the image of the city." When I asked an employee of the Ministry of Social Welfare her opinion on indigenous street vendors and beggars, she said, "It's terrible. I mean it totally affects the [urban] image. For starters, it's not sanitary to have these children here. I mean they perform their 'necessities' on the streets. They don't use a bathroom. So, already that decays the image. And to see begging children, who can just grab onto your leg and say 'please give me some change' and this and that . . . [she trailed off]" (June 3, 2003). Again, the emphasis is on cleanliness, hygiene, and the damaging aesthetic impact of indigenous bodies.

Much of this issue concerns social and spatial distancing. As stated by David Sibley, "portrayals of minorities as defiling and threatening have long been used to order society internally and to demarcate the boundaries of society, beyond which lie those who do not belong" (1995, 49). In this case, those who do not belong are "dirty Indian" children who urinate and perhaps defecate in public space. The issue is not the lack of public facilities for street workers but rather that they contaminate the streets and become threateningly close to middle-class government workers who are repulsed by their touch.

In Guayaquil similar discourses circulate. The new boardwalk is truly the city's prized gem. It is a manicured, sanitized boardwalk adjacent to the River Guayas. It has cafes, benches, gardens, and even a McDonalds. Yet the boardwalk is also guarded and monitored by heavily armed police during all opening hours. The gates close at midnight to prevent undesirables from sneaking in and spending the night. This boardwalk was designed with tourists and Guayaquil's upper and middle classes in mind. To keep it this way, in 2003 plans were underway to build a new boardwalk in the barrios or in the poorer suburbs of the city. According to the chief of police, it was being built because "On Saturdays and Sundays, you're sure to encounter a lot of people from the poorest barrios on the boardwalk. And this will make you suspicious or it'll give you a bad impression when there's only short people, ugly people, etc. So they're building a new boardwalk in the suburbs, where people can go without losing their merit, without losing their dignity, where they can mingle among themselves. It's just

easier that way" (July 1, 2003). In a classic example of social and spatial distancing, the plan is to keep the new boardwalk as striking as possible and free of
"short people" and "ugly people" (which can be understood as euphemisms for
the nonwhite and working class) and any other suspicious-looking individuals
who disrupt the image municipal authorities intend to project.

Race and ethnicity intersect all of these exclusionary strategies. Municipal
employees in Guayaquil spoke of the city's strong regionalism and disdain
for indigenous vendors and beggars. According to one woman, "it is because,
undoubtedly, indigenous people have hygienic customs that we on the coast
reject." When pressed further, she said that indigenous people "do not bathe"
and went on to talk about the differences between the ways blacks and Indians
smell (noting that blacks "have a special odor too, but it's not because they don't
bathe, it's because of their diet." Another woman in the same room suggested,
"it's also because of the color of their skin."). Trying to prove that they were not,
in fact, racists, they went on to talk about how much "admiration" they have
for Afro-Ecuadorians and how much they enjoy listening to their "voices" and
their "music." When I brought them back to the topic of indigenous people
from sierra, they again spoke of regionalism and said that people wish that
Indians would "go back to where they came from" (June 27, 2003).

In both Quito and Guayaquil, race, hygiene, and urban aesthetics have become intertwined to justify the displacement of indigenous street vendors and
beggars for the sake of tourism. Through everyday geographies of racism and
social exclusion, municipal rhetorics stress the need for purified urban spaces
free from the defiling effects of indigenous bodies. To maintain these purified
spaces, municipal authorities have invested in heightened police surveillance
and regulation to keep them clean.

Social Control and Regulation

Ecuador's hosting of the Miss Universe Pageant in 2004 speaks to its successful
reorientation toward tourism. During the broadcast of this event, carefully se-
lected and sanitized images of the nation were displayed to millions of viewers
around the world. The bulk of this event was hosted in Quito. Recognizing that
the global media was their captive audience, city leaders launched a publicity
campaign promoting Quito's beauty, cleanliness, order, and open arms to tourists (Pequeño 2004). This campaign went hand in hand with an attempt to cover
up the more unsightly parts of the city. In the months leading up to the pageant,
itinerant vendors and beggars complained of increasing police harassment and
arrests on the streets. The mayor denied these accusations and claimed that
these operatives had been in place for "several months" (which they likely had

been—the municipality had just started early). Refuting that beggars were being jailed, he said that elderly beggars were being brought to shelters to develop a "dignified life." But this was regardless of whether or not they were being brought and held against their will (*El Comercio* 2004a, 2004b).

Regulation and control are key parts of Quito and Guayaquil's neoliberal urban policies. Quito's chief of police described the regulation of itinerant workers as "a game of cat and mouse." Excessive regulation has forced vendors to hide in stores and doorways to avoid having their merchandise seized. These seizures are not uncommon; in fact, I witnessed vendors lose their goods on a number of occasions, during which items were clearly pocketed by the police for personal use. Quito's coordinator of Urban Management and Control does not deny that police take goods for their personal benefit but he insists that "they're not gluttons" (*El Comercio* 2003c). Because police officers are very underpaid, earning a mere $140 to $200 a month, corruption in these types of situations is common. In fact, Transparency International ranked Ecuador as one of the twelve most corrupt nations in the world (Wibbelsman 2003), a reality which my experiences in Ecuador certainly corroborate.

Many informal street workers complained of physical abuse at the hands of the police. One street outreach worker vehemently described how she observed police officers hit young male shoe shiners, seize their boxes, and forcibly remove them from Quito's historical center's plazas. In the same area she reported seeing an officer gas an elderly beggar and throw him to the ground. When hearing these claims, an urban planner made light of them and joked that "*el orden es de sacarlos a palos*," or the order is to remove them with sticks (September 2, 2003). Quito's main newspaper similarly reports abuses by the municipal police. One informal vendor was cited as saying, "They hit or throw gas at us men and they call women daughters of [whores]." Another said, "We have to hide like we're thieves" (*El Comercio* 2003d).

There has been much criticism concerning the social effects of these revitalization projects. Newspaper articles are replete with complaints from informal workers who denounce harassment and abuse at the hands of municipal police. Violence has played a larger role in the repression of informal street vendors in Guayaquil than in Quito. In 2003 alone the media reported ten cases of excessive police force in Guayaquil, many of which were captured on film (*El Universo* 2004a). One article describes a fifty-three-year-old man who was shot and severely injured during a forced eviction from an informal street market (*El Comercio* 2003a). These evictions were part of the municipality's attempt to move informal workers into organized markets "where they'll be more comfortable" (July 1, 2003). While admitting that a "few" police have violated procedures (*El Comercio* 2003b), the chief of police recognized that "unfortunately, the role of the police . . . has always been more repressive than preventative" (July 1, 2003).

In Guayaquil informal workers are by no means permitted in the regenerated areas of the city. At nights the streets are patrolled by truckloads of young, heavily armed police officers on the lookout for any signs of trouble (see Garcés 2004). A new municipal ordinance also allows for and in fact encourages private surveillance to play a role in the regulation of informal workers in the regenerated area.[2] This places the rights and interests of property owners above those of informal workers and all those who are perceived to violate subjective notions of "proper moral conduct" and "decor" (as outlined in the ordinance). To protect the city center for tourists and the middle class, spaces are being increasingly sanitized of troublesome images of poverty. As stated by the head of municipal operatives for the metropolitan police, informal workers in the municipality's tourist spots are "definitely a problem" (July 1, 2003).

The Comité Permanente por la Defensa de los Derechos Humanos (Permanent Committee for the Defense of Human Rights) has denounced Guayaquil's police for arresting five minors between the ages of nine and sixteen years of age (*El Comercio* 2003a). According to the director of Guayaquil's Programa del Muchacho Trabajador (Program for the Working Child), these boys and girls were arrested for cleaning windshields and selling water and candies, and held for five days in an adult cell (July 30, 2003). When I inquired about this, the chief of police admitted that they have detained "many minors" but stressed that most are "drug addicts" or "prostitutes" (July 1, 2003). While it is true that a number of children have substance abuse problems, a much larger number of children labor daily on the streets—their only crime being the occupation of public space.

For example, Héctor is a twelve-year-old indigenous Calhuaseño who has spent much time on the streets of Guayaquil and Quito. Héctor's most recent job in Guayaquil was as an itinerant cola vendor; he wandered the streets selling cola to pedestrians for ten cents a cup. But the municipality has cracked down on this activity with particular rigor. Targeted because their consumers litter plastic cups throughout the streets, cola vendors are now subject to a five-hundred-dollar fine and up to seven days in prison if caught working in the regenerated area. According to the mayor, itinerant cola vending causes "mess and chaos—and that's what I don't want" (*El Comercio* 2003b).

In July 2003 a group of Héctor's friends and family were arrested in Guayaquil. His grandmother, four of his aunts, and a group of others from his rural indigenous community were imprisoned for seven days for begging and selling gum. When his relatives were seized, one six-year-old boy managed to escape to inform his relatives what had happened. Had he not run away, he would have been imprisoned along with the community's women because, as the chief of police said, "if we can, then logically children are [detained] with their mothers" (July 1, 2003).

Because of the increasing levels of municipal harassment, many women and children from Héctor's community have decided to become involved in more risky transnational migration to beg on the streets of Colombia. According to one woman, "They treat us a hundred percent better than in Quito. [In Quito] people insult us, they don't give us money, and they don't buy from us. In Colombia, no. In Colombia, people are good. They give clothes to our children; they buy from us. People aren't bad there. It's much better" (July 6, 2006). However, their treatment by the Colombian authorities differs radically from that of the public. In fact, several women have had their young children temporarily seized by the Colombian authorities, much like what happened in Quito in 1999. Because they travel to Colombia with no documentation, speak Spanish poorly, and represent a very low strata of society, they are accorded few rights in the city. In fact, in at least one case Colombian authorities threatened to put an indigenous woman's child up for adoption because, like many indigenous women, she did not have her child's birth certificate. Authorities continued to refuse to return her son even after she obtained documentation because he was "too white" and thus couldn't possibly be hers. In the end her son was held by the Colombian authorities for eight days (July 6, 2006). The very fact that indigenous women and children are now willing to risk migration to the streets of Colombia speaks to the profound importance of the income they earn on the streets of Quito and Guayaquil.

Although tourists and visitors congratulate and commend the municipality for the work it has done to "clean up" the city, an assistant director at the Instituto Nacional del Niño y la Familia (National Institute for Children and Families) in Guayas does not agree: "I mean honestly, what's happening in my city, it's like putting makeup on a face and making it pretty when the liver is in bad shape, the kidneys are bad, and the heart has paralysis. Few of these people have seen the outskirts of the city. [If they did] they'd see that not much has been done. There are still sectors of the city that don't have water, that lack basic services. But we're investing a ton of money to cover up only the things we can see" (June 26, 2003). This cover-up of unsightly visual blemishes—including indigenous bodies—represents a particularly racialized version of the revanchist city. While tourism is deemed a savior for Ecuador's economic woes, at the moment it is doing very little to help those in the poorest sector of Ecuador's economy—namely indigenous street vendors and beggars.

Displacing the Indian in the "Modern" City

As Loic Wacquant notes about Brazil, New York–styled neoliberal penalization is "all the more seductive as well as all the more nefarious when it is applied to countries traversed by deep inequalities" (2003, 198). In Ecuador the implementation of revanchist urban policies has served only to exacerbate existing racial-spatial divides. The mere presence of "dirty Indians," "short people," and "ugly people" in tourist areas threatens to betray the nation's Indianness and backwardness to the world. Consequently, a particular imperative for Ecuadorian revanchism is to push these individuals beyond the city limits and back into the hidden folds of the Andes.

Quito and Guayaquil's neoliberal urban policies are effectively erasing spaces for the poor and working class while creating spaces for global tourists. The policies are promoted through carefully constructed notions of civic pride and accompanied by reduced freedoms, enhanced surveillance, and an increasing number of privatized spaces that are accessible to few. Guayaquil in particular has justified its revanchist urban policies through the defense of an imagined collective urban identity known as *guayaquileñidad*, an essentialist and regional construction of identity that allows little room for Indians (who should "go back to where they came from"). In fact, as Xavier Andrade (2005) points out, there is much irony in Guayaquil's civic pride campaign, popularized under the slogan *Más Ciudad* (More City). Although this slogan implies more city space for everyone, it in fact results in *Menos Ciudad* (Less City) for the majority.

In the end Ecuador's punitive neoliberal urban policies are only displacing troubling social problems. By constructing city space as a sanitized space for tourism and global capital, Guayaquil and Quito's urban regeneration campaigns merely turn attention away from the pressing social problems forcing indigenous peoples onto the streets in the first place. Rather, they merely displace them in an out of sight, out of mind mentality. Yet their problems persist—thus forcing some to engage in more dangerous activities, such as transnational migration. Ecuador's efforts to "save" children resonate with legislative attempts elsewhere. For instance, in 1993 U.S. legislators imposed an importation ban on products made by individuals under fifteen years of age. The unforeseen result of this was that at least fifty thousand South Asian children lost their factory jobs and were forced into more hazardous occupations, including prostitution (Ruddick 2003). While national level efforts in Ecuador are premised on child protection, they serve merely to appease people's consciences by removing troubling signs of poverty from the streets. Nothing is done to alleviate the larger structural forces (such as poverty, unemployment, and agricultural decline) pushing them into the streets to begin with.

As argued by Slater (2006), a critical focus on displacement is largely absent in current literature on gentrification and urban restructuring. This chapter has revealed how Ecuador's version of revanchism has encouraged blatant racial displacement. However, the individuals in this research are not being displaced from their homes (Newman and Wyly 2006; Slater 2004), but rather from their livelihoods (see Curran 2004). In fact, these revanchist urban policies are recasting the politics of national space by pushing rural-to-urban migrants into more risky transnational migration. This finding highlights how the importation of New York–styled neoliberal urban policies can result in harsher consequences for the most marginalized of people—particularly when local contexts include profound racial and economic inequality. It provides empirical evidence of how the diffusion of neoliberal urban policies from the Global North to the Global South can worsen the life conditions of the poor. By drawing attention to this issue, I hope to help revive critical perspectives on displacement both in the North and South.

In conclusion, this chapter provides an example of the differentiated ways in which revanchism takes shape in the South, thus furthering geographic debates surrounding the revanchist city. Ecuador's reorientation toward global tourism is founded on a hygienic racism that deepens preexisting racial-spatial divides and substantiates Smith's (2001) fear that the New York model would become a global template for postliberal revanchism. Indeed, these harsh neoliberal urban policies have diffused to Ecuador's largest cities—even though political, social, and economic conditions vary dramatically from those in the North—where they are being enacted in a particularly repressive and racialized form.

Conclusion

Begging as a Path to Progress

Shortly before leaving Ecuador in 2003, I was sitting in my kitchen with a fourteen-year-old girl named Malena, when she posed a difficult and troubling question. We were looking at pictures and chatting about the community when she said to me, "We work like donkeys but we don't make any money." Then she looked at me inquisitively and asked, "Why do other people have so much money?" I must admit that I struggled to answer Malena's question; my immediate response was to pull out a map and a magazine and begin pointing at pictures in an attempt to illustrate the inequitable distribution of wealth and power throughout the world. But despite my best efforts, my abstract explanation meant little to her. For many, it would seem logical to equate hard work with profits. This is supposed to be one of the mainstays of a capitalist economy. Yet things are different in Malena's community. No matter how hard they toil on their lands, they cannot make enough money to live. After having spent much time in Quito (and interacting with gringos like myself), Malena recognizes the dramatic incongruities between her life experiences and those of others.

For Malena and her peers, begging has become an effective way to overcome dire conditions of poverty and amend some of the inequities they encounter in the city. Ironic though it is, begging is helping youth get ahead, both in an educational and material sense. But despite its effectiveness, begging is a less than ideal way to attain this progress. Young people perceive it as a short-term strategy, which they hope will be discarded once they have attained some of their material and educational goals—or at least until they have found "something better." Growing up in this era of increasing global complexity presents many challenges for these indigenous youth and, unfortunately, these challenges may not become any easier in the years to come.

In this book I have tried to unravel a tale of what happens when modernization meets globalization. For many indigenous communities, globalization and the present-day neoliberal agenda have only exacerbated already difficult conditions. However, for the indigenous community of Calhuasí, the effects of globalization have been rather limited because, until recently, the community operated largely outside of the dominant market economy. In Calhuasí the key catalyst for recent change was the construction of the community's road in 1992. For the first time, community members—particularly women and children—became more closely connected to a world outside of their community. Not only did outsiders have ease of entrance, but community members also had ease of exit. The road facilitated the entrance of new building materials, propane tanks, and material consumer goods—all of which have had dramatic effects on the community. Consequently, during the most recent phase of globalization, Calhuaseños have not become poorer but rather have developed a heightened sense of their comparative poverty.

Within the context of these changes, children from Calhuasí aspire to futures that are different from those of their parents. They do not want to be agriculturalists, nor do they want big families. Rather, influenced by their experiences in the city and by media representations, they want to be doctors, teachers, pop stars, and police officers. They want big houses, trucks, and televisions. They want to be well educated so that they can attain some of these possibilities. Yet there are conflicting processes and ideologies in the community. While some parents have equally high aspirations for their children, others perceive little value in children's education. Through the media, teachers, and interactions in the city, children are being told that their proper place is in school and recreation. Meanwhile, within their community, they are being told that they must work. There are also real financial demands that mean that children have to work if they want to attend school or even hope to participate in consumer culture.

Children from Calhuasí deviate from current understandings of street and working children. These children are not from single-parent families and are not at risk of becoming homeless street children, largely because they work on the streets with their extended family members as part of tightly knit kinship groups. They are under constant surveillance by their aunts, uncles, cousins, grandmothers, parents, and/or siblings, who collectively are capable of exerting high levels of social control. Currently, children who work on the streets with their families are categorized with common conceptualizations of street and working children, despite their substantially different circumstances. While this research is specific to Ecuador, I suspect that family-based networks on the streets—particularly among rural migrants—are not so uncommon elsewhere. It could be that this group has been overlooked because of methodological difficulties concerning access and perhaps because of more pressing concerns for homeless street children. However, as a result the lives of these children have been misrepresented.

Contrary to the current literature on street and working children, the majority of Calhuaseño children involved in begging and gum vending are actually girls. This has much to do with Andean gender ideologies, which perceive few negative moral implications for girls on the streets. Traditionally, Andean girls and boys have been involved in both reproductive and productive work. However, as urban gender ideologies infiltrate the community through education, media, and migration, gender roles are shifting. Witness, for example, the profound imposition of gender constructs suggested by one of Calhuasí's schoolteachers: girls could be secretaries and housewives; boys could be mechanics. Perhaps recognizing these gender constructs (which suggest the submission and dependence of women), indigenous women and girls are much more likely to beg than men or boys. Boys may beg as long as they appear childlike; as they approach the age threshold of twelve to fourteen, they carry babies or toddlers to legitimize their involvement in begging. Because girls are more proficient at begging, they are more likely to be enrolled in school at a later age, withdrawn from school temporarily, or withdrawn from school permanently to support their siblings' educations.

In general, children's work in the city actually enables their further education. Out of those currently enrolled in school, almost 60 percent explicitly said that they work to pay for school supplies. Although there is not yet a single high school graduate from the community, a small group of youth is currently determined to get a high school diploma. Their work and their siblings' work on the streets is the only way they can afford to continue with their education. The finding that children's work on the streets is an *enabling* factor for their education runs contrary to common beliefs that child labor forces children to abandon school. It suggests that people should not be so hasty to condemn children's work on the streets and should instead recognize some of the positive outcomes of their work.

For girls the situation is a bit more complicated. Many desperately want to be educated. As twelve-year-old Monica told me, "I can go, I better go, and I will finish high school." At age twenty-one, Monica's oldest sister has little education. However, her sixteen-year-old sister, Isabel, is one of the few students enrolled in Quisapincha's high school. Her oldest sister's work in the city helps to pay for Isabel's schooling. Although Monica is behind by two grades in school owing to her work in the city, it is this work that allows her to carry on with her education. Therefore, while girls currently do not have the same access to education as boys, this may change from sheer determination. In fact, education is one of the reasons why many girls declared that they do not want to marry until they are in their twenties—an age much later than normal in the community.

Within a racist and sexist social structure, indigenous girls and young women are very limited in their employment options. On the streets they are frequently offered positions as domestic workers—an occupation deemed appropriate for young indigenous women within Ecuador's social and racial hierarchies. However, this occupation has been shown to expose girls to high levels of physical, psychological, and sexual abuse. Confined within strangers' homes, they receive low pay, endure limited freedom, and remain isolated from their friends and families. Begging and gum vending are thus alternative employment options for young indigenous girls—options that allow them to retain their freedom, continue to live with their families, earn substantially more money, and continue with their educational goals.

With this book, I hope to both counteract the paucity of knowledge concerning girls' involvement with street work and advance geographic understandings of gendered interactions with public space (see Katz 1993; Cresswell 1996; Ruddick 1996a; Valentine 1996; Yeoh and Huang 1998). I argue that street begging and gum vending are viable and possibly safer alternative employment options for indigenous girls. The girls I spoke with would prefer to beg and sell gum, both morally degraded activities, rather than be confined within a white-mestizo's home as a domestic worker and lose their freedom and their ability to study. Research elsewhere has suggested that there are few girls on the streets because they are more likely to find employment in the private sphere as domestic workers. My research, on the other hand, has described a group of girls who are more likely to work on the streets owing to indigenous gender constructs and a general rejection of domestic employment. This finding allows for a more nuanced understanding of the circumstances surrounding indigenous girls' involvement in street work.

As young indigenous women become more involved in rural-to-urban migration, they are shifting the markers of cultural identity—something previously reserved for men. By wearing nontraditional clothes, such as city skirts, baseball caps, and pants, they are identifying themselves as participants in the modern nation and the consumer economy. Consequently, indigenous girls are challenging what it means to be an indigenous woman in the Andes. However, these girls are also internalizing dominant racist discourses, which suggest that to be white is to belong to the nation. These racist discourses have profound effects on their understandings of themselves and their positions within Ecuador's social and racial hierarchies.

While indigenous women and children are constructed as "lazy Indians" who "prefer to sit and beg," children are often perceived to be on the streets because of "bad parenting" and manufactured necessity rather than actual poverty. Deviating from dominant understandings of 'proper' childhood, their very presence on the streets leads many to decry that they will inevitably become delinquents, criminals, and drug addicts. Within this discourse, attention is drawn away from problems associated with market economies that fail to redistribute wealth to the poor and rather focuses on the vices and alleged "laziness" of beggars themselves. Constructing beggars in this way thus justifies attempts to remove them from the streets.

Indigenous women and children's exclusion from the urban sphere is further justified through ideological constructions of space, urban revitalization, and the push for global tourism. When city space is reserved for tourism and global capital, rural Indians begging on street corners are perceived to disrupt the meaning of this space. A discourse of purity and defilement is then evoked wherein beggars are said to offend and disturb the image of a "Clean Quito" or "Twenty-First-Century Guayaquil." Thus, by divorcing the matter of begging from a wider context, the issue becomes more about removing indigenous women and children from the streets (framed in the common-sense discourse that "the streets are no place for a child," for example) than about trying to alleviate the larger forces that push them there in the first place.

Social and spatial distancing of the unwanted "other" is a dominant theme in this book. In a particularly potent example, Guayaquil's chief of police discussed the municipal intent to keep the new boardwalk free of "short people" and "ugly people" so that tourists and members of the upper and middle classes could enjoy the boardwalk without feeling "suspicious" or having "bad impressions." The municipality intends to build a new boardwalk in the suburbs so that these "short" and "ugly" people can go "without losing their dignity" to "mingle among themselves." Many Guayaquileños wish that begging indigenous women and children would "go back to where they came from," thus suggesting a particularly racialized form of social exclusion.

Herein, I have also provided an example of the differentiated ways in which revanchism takes shape in the South. In Ecuador harsh neoliberal urban policies are being diffused to its largest cities, where conditions vary significantly from those in the Global North. This is particularly the case in Guayaquil, where Plan Bratton has led to a crackdown on beggars, informal workers, street children, homosexuals, transvestites, and the (largely nonwhite) working class. Ecuador's particular twist on this New York–styled penalization is its more transparent engagement with the process of blanqueamiento. In a nation traversed by deep social and racial inequalities, this is a disturbing prospect.

However, far from being passive victims, women and children have learned to rework oppressive conditions to confront, resist, and even assume essentialized roles in the city. Of particular interest here is child "renting." Indigenous children belong to economies of caring that deviate from the dominant norm. Children are often cared for, for months and even years at a time, by members of their extended families. Loaning children and informal adoptions are long-standing practices in Andean communities. These arrangements often serve as apprenticeships and are tied to the redistribution of wealth between community members. By sending children to the city with their relatives, parents allow children to get to know the city, learn how to earn income, and become more productive contributors to the family. It also temporarily relieves parents of some of their child care responsibilities and brings in much needed financial income. Community members do not believe that they are renting children; rather, they refer to this practice as "loaning" or "sending" children. Yet they continue to be criticized by NGO workers and authorities for practicing models of childhood and parenting that deviate from the standard norm.

For women and children from Calhuasí, begging and gum vending have evolved to become more than mere survival strategies. They have become crucial activities for further education, consumption, and participation in the world outside of their community. However, while community members may use their earnings to build big houses and buy trucks, by no means are they now wealthy. Rather, ironic though it is, begging is an activity that is allowing them to move forward within the confines of a capitalist market economy. Unwilling to sit on the sidelines or be left behind, they have actively engaged in an activity that may allow them to eventually attain some of their material and personal goals.

While the impact of globalization is far-reaching, it is important to note its mitigated effects at varied spatial scales. Calhuasí is a community where the processes of economic globalization have had limited influence; rather, the community is undergoing processes that are more closely aligned to modernization. Within a capitalist understanding of modernization, the community is "developing." Community members are purchasing material commodities, building more modern houses, and becoming educated. However, Calhuasí's modernization has taken a particular form. Within ideologies of capitalist modernization, hard work is deemed crucial for progress. On the contrary, begging is associated with decay and stagnation. It is ironic then that Calhuaseños have capitalized on begging as an effective path to progress. This is highly counterintuitive and brings attention to the differentiated ways in which modernization and globalization take shape in a marginalized region of the periphery.

Surprisingly, there has been very little research published in English on beggars in regions of the Global South or on women and children who beg. There seems to be a belief, carried over from the Global North, that giving money to beggars only aggravates the situation (i.e., "Your help doesn't help me"). Diverted-giving campaigns are common across cities and advocate donating to organized charities to protect beggars "from their own vices." Curiously, this ideological stance has been unproblematically applied to child beggars in Ecuador, when there is no empirical evidence to suggest that giving to child beggars destroys their lives. In fact, my research suggests the opposite: instead of destroying their lives, begging and gum sales are enabling possibilities that they have never had before—such as education, better housing, bicycles, trucks, and participation in a world outside of their community.

What may be the larger issue for policy makers and child advocates is that on the streets the "purity" and "innocence" of childhood appears defiled. Describing children as being "confined to a little piece of sidewalk" is powerful imagery that contravenes idyllic images of children whose "purpose in life is to smile." But institutionalizing, diverting giving, or seizing children does little to actually help their real economic needs. Rather, it merely covers up these "dirty" racialized children and attempts to push them back to the countryside where Indians are deemed to belong. Antibegging campaigns should be approached critically, and the ideological underpinnings and empirical evidence for their claims should be examined.

Finally, this book is a call to planners, policy makers, and social workers to consider the complex and varied factors that push marginalized families onto the streets. Rather than relying on problematic stereotypes of parents as "drunks" or "bad mothers," individuals must understand the many factors that lead to street work. Pushing indigenous women and children beyond city boundaries or back to the countryside is a short-term "solution" at best; it merely displaces indigenous women and children temporarily. As stated by Quito's chief of police, "They always return" (August 5, 2003)—largely because their problems persist. Municipalities and the state should work together to invest in rural areas, create sources of employment, establish fair prices for agriculture, and improve access to education. For young people, scholarship programs would greatly enhance youth graduation rates, particularly at the high school level. Part-time schools, such as the one attended by Leo, would allow young people to further their education while working in the city. Undeniably, the best solution would be to overcome the systemic racism that plagues Ecuador's indigenous peoples, which is no small task. The problems faced by rural indigenous peoples are overwhelming and unfortunately will not be solved overnight. Yet the struggle must continue so that young people can find futures that truly involve "something better."

NOTES

Introduction

1. Calhuasí has a population of approximately 1,250, divided among 255 families.

2. I use the term *racialized* in the context of racialization—a racist ideology that establishes biological, physical, hygienic, cultural, and/or environmental hierarchies used to exclude individuals and groups (see Barot and Bird 2001).

3. This case is also true for many poorer regions of the Global North. See Bourgois (2003) for a disturbing account of how impoverished U.S. youth grow up in Harlem.

4. See Hecht (1998, 70–92) for an example of how these modern constructions play out in Brazil.

5. The category of mestizo signifies a racial and cultural mix between whites, blacks, and indigenous peoples. White-mestizo is used to describe those who self-identify as white, most of whom are among the nation's elite.

Chapter 1. Ecuador

All names in this text are pseudonyms.

1. Not all migrants on the streets are indigenous, of course, yet the majority of street vendors and beggars are nonwhite (indigenous, mestizo, or Afro-Ecuadorian). While I focus particularly on indigenous street vendors and beggars in this book, many of the arguments presented here also apply to Afro-Ecuadorians.

2. Ecuador's statistics have only recently begun to be disaggregated by language (i.e., Quichua or Spanish), which allows some approximation of figures for indigenous peoples.

3. All interviews were recorded and translated from Spanish by the author.

4. See Powers (1995) for a historical analysis of how indigenous peoples used to avoid identification as Indians to evade tribute payments and draft labor during the colonial period.

5. There are many variants to the spelling of Calhuasí including Calguasig, Calhuasig, Calguasí, and Calohuasí.

6. For a critical analysis of the Comuna Law, see Becker (1999).

7. There are no telephone landlines but cell phones are becoming increasingly popular. Because the communities are high in the mountains, reception is often quite good but the cost of making calls is prohibitively high.

8. The Latin names for these Andean root crops are *Ullucus tuberosus*, *Tropaeolum tuberosum*, and *Oxalis tuberosa*, respectively (CESA 2002).

9. By comparison, Ecuador's population growth rate during the same period was 1.03 percent (CIA 2004).

10. In 1996 inflation was 24.4 percent. Over the subsequent years, it rose substantially to peak in 2000—the year of dollarization—30.6 percent in 1997; 36.1 percent in 1998; 52.2 percent in 1999; 96.1 percent in 2000; 37.7 percent in 2001 (SIISE 2003i).

11. A Spanish quintal is approximately 46 kilograms or 101 pounds.

Chapter 2. Indigenous Childhoods

1. The part-time high school offers classes every Saturday. Although several individuals attend this high school, it is criticized for having low educational standards.

2. La Tola Shelter, known as the Hospedería Campesina La Tola, was a shelter for indigenous migrants. It was run by Salesian priests and social workers between 1973 and 2003. It closed in 2003 because the municipality would not renew their lease, largely because of concerns that they were encouraging begging in the city. A new shelter, the Hospedería Campesina Don Bosco Chillogallo (Don Bosco Chillogallo Campesino Shelter), has since been constructed, but its location on the far outskirts of the city means that few migrants use it. They now rent rooms in the central city instead. The Fundación Don Bosco, my gatekeeper for this research, was created in 2002 as a response to the impending closure of La Tola Shelter.

3. The sisters earned their livings as guardians of the *Libro de San Gonzolo*, a witch's book reputed to control life and death. By paying the guardians of the witch's book a hefty sum, individuals are able to access San Gonzalo's evil powers to harm their enemies. The most critical act for activating this witchcraft is to have the intended victim's name and manner of death or misfortune written into San Gonzolo's book (Wogan 2004). The only way to avoid or stop this witchcraft is to pay the guardians. Unfortunately for these particular guardians, their involvement in Calhuasí coincided with a tuberculosis outbreak. No matter how much money community members paid them, people continued to die—resulting in a death toll of more than forty (*Diario Hoy* 1996b; Tibanlombo 1996; Guerrero 2001).

4. At the time of this research, there were approximately 324 women between the ages of twelve and forty-five in the community. However, the majority of young women do not have children until at least sixteen years old and some women continue to have children after age forty-five. Taking this into account, out of these 324 women, fewer than 4 percent of women of child-bearing age use IUDs. If we calculate for women between the ages of eighteen and forty-five, the figure rises to fewer than 6 percent.

5. During my time in Ecuador, I attended two Calhuaseño weddings. The brides were fourteen and fifteen years old, while the grooms were sixteen and seventeen. I also met a woman in Calhuasí who was the same age as I—twenty-nine at the time. After chatting, we discovered that we were both married but she had married seventeen years earlier, when she was twelve years old. She had married an eleven-year-old boy.

6. Quisapincha Alto's schools do have a small handful of computers but these are primarily reserved for use by teachers.

Chapter 3. Migrant Childhoods

1. An outreach worker at the Centro de la Niña Trabajadora (Center for the Working Girl) believes the number could be as low as thirty, whereas according to Castelnuovo and Associates there are approximately a thousand street children in Quito in 2000 (Castelnuovo y Asociados 2002, 58). These wide discrepancies are likely due to the ways in which street children are both defined and counted.

2. This figure was calculated in response to the question, "Where do you work?" The survey was conducted by DNI-Ecuador in 1994 and aggregated by SIISE.

3. This survey was conducted in 1997 in both Quito and Guayaquil and reports a confidence level of 95 percent.

4. I have seen a few cases where young children have been left unsupervised on sidewalks or at intersections but these instances are relatively rare.

5. If lights change every four minutes, they must sell a pack of gum at every other light change. I was unable to calculate profit margins for those who sell Halls, Clorets, or Trident products. Initially, only a few individuals were selling these products; however, shortly before I left this number skyrocketed.

Chapter 4. Antibegging Rhetoric

1. This is with the exception of beggars from ethnic minority groups such as Gypsy Travelers or Romas (see Gmelch 1979; Helleiner 2003).

2. For instance, individuals sixty-five years old and above who worked outside of the formal sector (such as in agriculture or in street sales) are entitled to $7.50 per month through the Bono Solidario (Solidarity Bonus). Disabled individuals are also entitled to this amount. Considering that in 2006 the basic budget (*canasta básica*) for an average urban family was calculated at approximately $450.00 per month, which would cover minimum food and household expenses (INEC 2006), this supplement is very low.

3. Mingas are the norm in Calhuasí. Among other indigenous groups they are no longer as important or as regular, perhaps because community members have become more integrated into the capitalist economy.

Chapter 5. Race, Space, and the City

1. The Proyecto de Ley de Protección para Niños, Niñas y Adolescentes Indigentes (24-003) bill was presented by Diputado Marco Proaño Maya to the National Congress of Ecuador on January 6, 2003.

2. Ordenanza Reglamentaria de la Zona de Regeneración Urbana del Centro de la Ciudad, Municipalidad de Guayaquil, arts. 12.2 and 16 (January 14, 2004), Registro Oficial 234, *Ordenanza de Regeneración Urbana para la Ciudad de Guayaquil*.

REFERENCES

Aitken, Stuart. 2001. *Geographies of young people: The morally contested spaces of identity.* New York: Routledge.

Andrade, Xavier. 2005. "Más ciudad," menos ciudadanía: Renovación urbana y aniquilación del espacio público en Guayaquil. In *Regeneración y revitalización urbana en las Américas: Hacia un estado estable*, ed. F. Carrión and L. Hanley, 147–168. Quito: FLACSO/Woodrow Wilson International Center for Scholars.

Anthias, Floya, and Nira Yuval-Davis. 1992. *Racialized boundaries: Race, nation, gender, colour and class and the anti-racist struggle.* New York: Routledge.

Appadurai, Arjun. 1990. Disjuncture and difference in the global cultural economy. *Theory, Culture & Society* 7:295–310.

Aptekar, Lewis, and Behailu Abebe. 1997. Conflict in the neighbourhood: Street and working children in the public space. *Childhood* 4:477–490.

Ariès, Philippe. 1962. *Centuries of childhood.* New York: Knopf.

Atkinson, Rowland. 2003. Domestication by cappuccino or a revenge on urban space? Control and empowerment in the management of public spaces. *Urban Studies* 40:1829–1843.

Barot, Rohit, and John Bird. 2001. Racialization: The genealogy and critique of a concept. *Ethnic and Racial Studies* 24:601–618.

Beazley, Harriot. 1999. "A little but enough": Street children's subcultures in Yogyakarta, Indonesia. PhD diss., Australian National Univ.

———. 2002. "Vagrants wearing make-up": Negotiating spaces on the streets of Yogyakarta, Indonesia. *Urban Studies* 39:1665–1683.

Bebbington, Anthony. 2000. Reencountering development: Livelihood transitions and place transformation in the Andes. *Annals of the Association of American Geographers* 90:495–520.

Becker, Marc. 1999. Comunas and indigenous protest in Cayambe, Ecuador. *Americas* 55:531–559.

———. 2008. *Indians and leftists in the making of Ecuador's modern indigenous movement.* Durham, N.C.: Duke Univ. Press.

Belina, Bernd, and Gesa Helms. 2003. Zero tolerance for the industrial past and other threats: Policing and urban entrepreneurialism in Britain and Germany. *Urban Studies* 40:1845–1867.

Belote, James, and Linda S. Belote. 1984. Suffer the little children: Death, autonomy, and responsibility in a changing "low technology" environment. *Science, Technology & Human Values* 9:35–48.

Bonnet, Michel. 1993. Child labor in Africa. *International Labor Review* 132:371–384.

Bonnett, Alastair. 2000. *White identities: Historical and international perspectives.* London: Prentice Hall.

Bourgois, Philippe. 2003. *In search of respect: Selling crack in El Barrio.* New York: Cambridge Univ. Press.

Bowling, Benjamin. 1999. The rise and fall of New York murder: Zero tolerance or crack's decline? *British Journal of Criminology* 39:531–554.

Bradshaw, York W., Rita Noonan, Laura Gash, and Claudia Buchmann Sershen. 1993. Borrowing against the future: Children and Third World indebtedness. *Social Forces* 71:629–656.

Bromley, Rosemary, and Gareth Jones. 1995. Conservation in Quito: Policies and progress in the historic centre. *Third World Planning Review* 17:41–60.

Camacho Muñoz, Miguel. 1991. *Diagnóstico de las Parroquias Pasa, Quisapincha, y San Fernando (Cantón Ambato, Provincia Tungurahua), en el objetivo de seleccionar una nueva área para el trabajo de CESA.* Quito: CESA.

Capello, Ernesto. 2005. City fragments: Space and nostalgia in modernizing Quito, 1885–1942. PhD diss., Univ. of Texas at Austin, Dept. of History.

Castelnuovo y Asociados. 2002. *Informe del rapid assessment aplicado a niñas en trabajo agrícola, doméstico, y explotación sexual.* Quito: OIT-IPEC.

CESA (Centro Ecuatoriano de Servicios Agrícolas). 1992. *Prediagnóstico participativo de las organizaciones campesinas de las Parroquias de Quisapincha, Pasa, y San Fernando.* Quito: CESA.

———. 1995. *Proyecto "Desarrollo de las organizaciones campesinas de la parte alta de Quisapincha."* Quito: CESA.

———. 2002. *Plan de manejo definitivo actual: Proyecto Quisapincha.* Ambato, Ecuador: CESA.

Chango Ruiz, Estuardo. 1993. *Diagnóstico externo comunal: Calguasig Grande.* Unpublished document produced for PROMUTA-CARE International, Ambato, Ecuador.

Chaudhuri, Sumita. 1987. *Beggars of Kalighat Calcutta.* Calcutta: Anthropological Survey of India.

Chossudovsky, Michel. 1997. *The globalization of poverty: Impacts of IMF and World Bank reforms.* London: Zed Books.

CIA (Central Intelligence Agency). 2004. The world factbook 2004: Ecuador. http://www.odci.gov/cia/publications/factbook/geos/ec.html (accessed December 4, 2003).

———. 2008. The world factbook 2008: Ecuador. https://www.cia.gov/library/publications/the-world-factbook/geos/ec.html (accessed October 7, 2008).

Clark, A. Kim. 1998. Race, "culture," and mestizaje: The statistical construction of the Ecuadorian nation, 1930–1950. *Journal of Historical Sociology* 11:185–211.

COCIQ (Corporación de Organizaciones Campesinas Indígenas de Quisapincha). 1999. *Plan de desarrollo local.* Quisapincha, Ecuador: COCIQ.

Colloredo-Mansfeld, Rudi. 1994. Architectural conspicuous consumption and economic change in the Andes. *American Anthropologist* 96:845–865.

———. 1998. "Dirty Indians," radical *indígenas*, and the political economy of social difference in modern Ecuador. *Bulletin of Latin American Research* 17:185–205.

———. 1999. *The native leisure class: Consumption and cultural creativity in the Andes.* Chicago: Univ. of Chicago Press.

El Comercio. 2002a. El comercio informal está fuera de control en Ambato. Quito. November 13, D4.

———. 2002b. Correo de lectores: Contrastes del Centro. Quito. October 18, A4.

———. 2002c. Mañana se elige a la nueva Reina. Quito. November 20, B8.

———. 2002d. Quito en emergencia y sin actividades. Quito. November 4, A3.

———. 2003a. 57 policías metropolitanos fueron echados. Quito. July 7. http://www.elcomercio.com/noticias.asp?noid=66250 (accessed July 19, 2004).

———. 2003b. La kola KR limitará sus ventas. Quito. May 31. http://www.elcomercio.com/noticias.asp?noid=62670&hl=true (accessed July 19, 2004).

———. 2003c. Los vendedores informales rebasan el control municipal. Quito. May 23. http://www.elcomercio.com/noticias.asp?noid=61876&hl=true (accessed July 19, 2004).

———. 2003d. Las ventas ambulantes crecen a pesar del control. Quito. December 23. http://www.elcomercio.com/noticias.asp?noid=81863 (accessed July 19, 2004).

———. 2004a. Entrevista: "No hay operativos especiales"; Paco Moncayo, alcalde del Distrito Metropolitano de Quito. Quito. May 12. http://www.elcomercio.com/noticias.asp?noid=93345 (accessed July 19, 2004).

———. 2004b. Las rutinas cambian con la llegada de las "misses." Quito. May 17. http://www.elcomercio.com/noticias.asp?noid=93780 (accessed July 19, 2004).

Congreso Nacional. 2003. *Código penal.* Quito: Editorial Jurídica del Ecuador.Cresswell, Tim. 1996. *In place/out of place: Geography, ideology, and transgression.* Minneapolis: Univ. of Minnesota Press.

Cruz, Alfredo, Víctor Hugo Fiallo, Eduardo Hinojoza, Ramiro Moncayo, Bolívar Rendón, and José Sola. 1994. *Participación y desarrollo campesino: El caso de San Fernando–Pasa-Quisapincha (síntesis).* Quito: CESA.

Curran, Winifred. 2004. Gentrification and the nature of work: Exploring the links in Williamsburg, Brooklyn. *Environment and Planning A* 36:1243–1258.

Daccach, Luis Alberto. 2003. Opinión pública: Los niños y sus derechos. Letter to the editor. *El Universo.* Guayaquil. June 26, 13A.

Dean, Hartley. 1999. *Begging questions. Street-level economic activity and social policy failure.* Bristol, England: Policy.

de la Cadena, Marisol. 1995. "Women are more Indian": Ethnicity and gender in a community near Cuzco. In *Ethnicity, markets, and migration in the Andes: At the crossroads of history and anthropology,* ed. B. Larson and O. Harris, 329–348. Durham, N.C.: Duke Univ. Press.

———. 2000. *Indigenous mestizos: The politics of race and culture in Cuzco, Peru, 1919–1991.* Durham, N.C.: Duke Univ. Press.

de la Torre, Carlos. 2000. Racism in education and the construction of citizenship in Ecuador. *Race & Class* 42:33–45.

———. 2002a. *Afroquiteños: Ciudadanía y racismo.* Quito: Centro Andino de Acción Popular.

———. 2002b. *El racismo en el Ecuador: Las experiencias de los indios de clase media.* Quito: Abya-Yala.

DeVerteuil, Geoffrey. 2006. The local state and homeless shelters: Beyond revanchism? *Cities* 23:109–120.

Diario Hoy. 1996a. Brujas saldrían en libertad. Ambato. August 20, 12B. Ambato.

———. 1996b. El castigo fue látigo y ortiga. Quito. July 22, 2A.

———. 1997a. Crece trabajo infantil. Quito. September 8, 2B. http://www.hoy.com.ec/ (accessed January 12, 2003).

———. 1997b. Ecuatoriano gana premio de periodismo. Quito. October 29. http://www.explored.com.ec (accessed January 31, 2005).

DMQ (Distrito Metropolitano de Quito). 2001. Proyecto Quito solidario y responsable con niños, niñas y adolescentes de la calle. http://www.quito.gov.ec/homequito/municipio/planxxi/Quitosolidario.htm (accessed March 5, 2002).

DNI-Ecuador (Defensa de Niñas y Niños Internacional). 1997. *Encuesta de opinión nacional a niños, niñas y jóvenes ecuatorianos entre 6 y 17 años de edad*. Mi opinión sí cuenta 22. Quito: DNI-Ecuador.

Doolittle, William E. 2001. Learning to see the impacts of individuals. *Geographical Review* 91:423–429.

Douglas, Mary. 1990. Foreward: No free gifts. In *The gift*, ed. M. Mauss, ix–xxii. London: Routledge.

Duncan, James. 1978. Men without property: The tramp's classification and use of urban space. *Antipode* 10:24–34.

Dyson, Jane. 2008. Harvesting identities: Youth, work, and gender in the Indian Himalayas. *Annals of the Association of American Geographers* 98:160–179.

Encalada, Eduardo, Fernando García, and Kristine Ivarsdotter. 1999. *La participación de los pueblos indígenas y negros en el desarrollo del Ecuador*. Washington D.C.: Unidad de Pueblos Indígenas y Desarrollo Comunitario, Banco Interamericano de Desarrollo, Departamento de Desarrollo Sostenible.

Erskine, Angus, and Ian McIntosh. 1999. Why begging offends: Historical perspectives and continuities. In Dean 1999, 27–42.

Fassin, Didier. 2001. The biopolitics of otherness: Undocumented foreigners and racial discrimination in French public debate. *Anthropology Today* 17:3–7.

Featherstone, Mike. 1990. Global culture: An introduction. *Theory, Culture & Society* 7:1–14.

Fitzpatrick, Suzanne, and Catherine Kennedy. 2001. The links between begging and rough sleeping: A question of legitimacy? *Housing Studies* 16:549–568.

FNA (Foro por la Niñez y Adolescencia). 2001. *Código de la niñez y adolescencia: ¡Apruébame!* Quito: Movimiento Social por los Derechos de los Niños, Niñas y Adolescentes, INNFA, Nuestros Niños.

———. 2002. *Código de la niñez y adolescencia: De la A a la Z*. Quito: MBS, Congreso Nacional del Ecuador, Pro Justicia, INNFA, Plan Internacional, UNICEF.

Fundación Natura. 2000. *Incremento de enfermedades respiratorias en escolares de Quito por contaminación atmosférica de origen vehicular*. Quito: Fundación Natura.

Garcés, Chris. 2004. Exclusión constitutiva: Las organizaciones pantalla y lo anti-social en la renovación urbana de Guayaquil. *Íconos* 20:43–63.

Gauderman, Kimberley. 2003. *Women's lives in colonial Quito: Gender, law, and economy in Spanish America.* Austin: Univ. of Texas Press.

Glauser, Benno. 1997. Street children: Deconstructing a construct. In James and Prout 1997, 145–164.

Gmelch, Sharon. 1979. *Tinkers and travellers.* Dublin, Ireland: O'Brien.

Guamán Poma de Ayala, Felipe, and David L. Frye. 2006. *The first new chronicle and good government,* abridged. Indianapolis: Hackett.

Guerrero, Andrés. 1997. The construction of a ventriloquist's image: Liberal discourse and the "miserable Indian race" in late 19th century Ecuador. *Journal of Latin American Studies* 29:555–590.

———. 2001. Los linchamientos en las comunidades indígenas: ¿La política perversa de una modernidad marginal? *Ecuador Debate* 53:197–226.

Halpern, Adam, and France Winddance Twine. 2000. Antiracist activism in Ecuador: Black-Indian community alliances. *Race & Class* 42:19–31.

Hamilton, Sarah. 1998. *The two-headed household: Gender and rural development in the Ecuadorean Andes.* Pittsburgh: Univ. of Pittsburgh Press.

Hansson, Desiree. 2003. "Strolling" as a gendered experience: A feminist analysis of young females in Cape Town. *Children, Youth and Environments* 13 (1). http://colorado .edu/journals/cye (accessed October 25, 2004).

Harcourt, Bernard. 2001. *Illusion of order: The false promise of broken windows policing.* Cambridge: Harvard Univ. Press.

Harvey, David. 1990. *The condition of postmodernity: An enquiry into the conditions of cultural change.* Cambridge, England: Blackwell.

Hecht, Tobias. 1998. *At home in the street: Street children of northeast Brazil.* Cambridge: Cambridge Univ. Press.

Helleiner, Jane. 2003. The politics of Traveller "child begging" in Ireland. *Critique of Anthropology* 23:17–33.

Hermer, Joe. 1999. Policing compassion: "Diverted giving" on the Winchester High Street. In Dean 1999, 203–218.

———. Forthcoming. *Policing compassion: Begging, law and power in public spaces.* Oxford: Hart.

Hermer, Joe, and Janet Mosher, eds. 2002. *Disorderly people: Law and the politics of exclusion in Ontario.* Halifax, Canada: Fernwood.

Holloway, Sarah L., and Gill Valentine. 2000. Children's geographies and the new social studies of childhood. In *Children's geographies: Playing, living, learning,* ed. S. Holloway and G. Valentine, 1–26. New York: Routledge.

Hopkins, Peter E. 2004. Young Muslim men in Scotland: Inclusions and exclusions. *Children's Geographies* 2:257–272.

La Hora. 2003. Una atención debe ser permanente: Celebración de la niñez ecuatoriana en sectores populares. Quito. June 2. http://www.lahora.com.ec (accessed June 2, 2003).

Hubbard, Phil. 2004. Revenge and injustice in the neoliberal city: Uncovering masculinist agendas. *Antipode* 36:665–686.

ILO (International Labor Organization). 2001. Indigenous people still the poorest of the poor. August 8. http://www.ilo.org/public/english/region/asro/bangkok/newsroom/pro105.htm (accessed December 30, 2004).

INEC (Instituto Nacional de Estadística y Censos). 2006. Índice de precios al consumidor urbano IPC—julio 2006. http://www.inec.gov.ec/ (accessed September 21, 2006).

INNFA (Instituto Nacional del Niño y la Familia). 2001. Programa de Protección y Educación del Niño Trabajador. http://www.innfa.org/programas/programas.html (accessed November 18, 2001).

Invernizzi, Antonella. 2003. Street working-children and adolescents in Lima: Work as an agent of socialization. *Childhood* 10:319–341.

Jaffe, Audrey. 1990. Detecting the beggar: Arthur Conan Doyle, Henry Mayhew, and "The Man with the Twisted Lip." *Representations* 31:96–117.

James, Allison, and Alan Prout, eds. 1997. *Constructing and reconstructing childhood: Contemporary issues in the sociological study of childhood.* Washington, D.C.: Falmer.

Jeffrey, Craig, Patricia Jeffery, and Roger Jeffery. 2008. *Degrees without freedom? Education, masculinity and unemployment in north India.* Stanford: Stanford Univ. Press.

Katz, Cindi. 1991. Sow what you know: The struggle for social reproduction in rural Sudan. *Annals of the Association of American Geographers* 81:488–514.

———. 1993. Growing girls/closing circles: Limits on the spaces of knowing in rural Sudan and U.S. cities. In *Full circles: Geographies of women over the life course*, ed. C. Katz and J. Monk, 88–106. New York: Routledge.

———. 1998. Disintegrating developments: Global economic restructuring and the eroding ecologies of youth. In *Cool places: Geographies of youth cultures*, ed. T. Skelton and G. Valentine, 130–144. New York: Routledge.

———. 2001. On the grounds of globalisation: A topography for feminist political engagement. *Signs* 4:1213–1234.

———. 2004. *Growing up global: Economic restructuring and children's everyday lives.* Minneapolis: Univ. of Minnesota Press.

Kilbride, Philip, Collette Suda, and Enos Njeru. 2000. *Street children in Kenya: Voices of children in search of a childhood.* Westport, Conn.: Bergin & Garvey.

Kingman, Eduardo. 2006. *La ciudad y los otros, Quito 1860–1940: Higienismo, ornato y policía.* Quito: FLACSO Sede Ecuador, Universidad Rovira e Virgili.

Korovkin, Tanya. 1997. Taming capitalism: The evolution of the indigenous peasant economy in northern Ecuador. *Latin American Research Review* 32:89–110.

Lankenau, Stephen E. 1999. Stronger than dirt: Public humiliation and status enhancement among panhandlers. *Journal of Contemporary Ethnography* 28:288–318.

Larrea, Carlos, Wilma B. Freire, and Chessa Lutter. 2001. *Equidad desde el principio: Situación nutricional de los niños ecuatorianos.* Washington D.C.: Organización Panamericana de la Salud.

Larrea, Carlos, and Liisa North. 1997. Ecuador: Adjustment policy impacts on truncated development and democratisation. *Third World Quarterly* 18:913–934.

Lawson, Victoria. 1999. Questions of migration and belonging: Understandings of migration under neoliberalism in Ecuador. *International Journal of Population Geography* 5:261–276.

Leinaweaver, Jessaca. 2008. *The circulation of children: Kinship, adoption, and morality in Andean Peru.* Durham, N.C.: Duke Univ. Press.

Lentz, Carola. 1997. *Migración e identidad étnica: La transformación histórica de una comunidad indígena en la Sierra Ecuatoriana.* Quito: Abya-Yala.

Lind, Amy. 2005. *Gendered paradoxes: Women's movements, state restructuring, and global development in Ecuador.* University Park: Penn State Press.

Lucchini, Riccardo. 1994. *The street girl: Prostitution, family and drug.* Working paper for English version of chapter 3 in forthcoming book *Entre la rue et la famille: L'enfant de Montevideo.* http://www.unifr.ch/socsem/Fichiers%20PDF/Wp243.pdf (accessed November 5, 2004).

Macleod, Gordon. 2002. From urban entrepreneurialism to a "revanchist city"? On the spatial injustices of Glasgow's renaissance. *Antipode* 34:602–624.

Macleod, Gordon, and Kevin Ward. 2002. Spaces of utopia and dystopia: Landscaping the contemporary city. *Geografiska Annaler* 84:153–170.

Mahtani, Minelle. 2002. Tricking the border guards: Performing race. *Environment and Planning D: Society and Space* 20:425–440.

Martínez Novo, Carmen. 2003. The "culture" of exclusion: Representations of indigenous women street vendors in Tijuana, Mexico. *Bulletin of Latin American Research* 22:249–268.

———. 2006. *Who defines indigenous? Identities, development, intellectuals, and the state in northern Mexico.* New Brunswick, N.J.: Rutgers Univ. Press.

Martínez Valle, Luciano. 2003. Endogenous peasant responses to structural adjustment: Ecuador in comparative Andean perspective. In *Rural progress, rural decay: Neoliberal adjustment policies and local initiatives,* ed. L. North and J. D. Cameron, 85–105. Bloomfield, N.J.: Kumarian.

Massey, Doreen. 1998. The spatial construction of youth cultures. In *Cool places: Geographies of youth cultures,* ed. T. Skelton and G. Valentine, 121–129. New York: Routledge.

Mauss, Marcel. 1966. *The gift: The form and reason for exchange in archaic societies.* Trans. Ian Cunnison. London: Cohen & West.

MBS (Ministerio de Bienestar Social). 2003. *Código de la Niñez y Adolescencia.* Quito: Gráficas Iberia.

Middleton, Alan. 2003. Informal traders and planners in the regeneration of historic city centres: The case of Quito, Ecuador. *Progress in Planning* 59:71–123.

Miles, Ann. 1994. Helping out at home: Gender socialization, moral development and devil stories in Cuenca, Ecuador. *Ethos* 22:132–157.

———. 2000. Poor adolescent girls and social transformations in Cuenca, Ecuador. *Ethos* 28:54–74.

Milton, Cynthia E. 2005. Poverty and the politics of colonialism: "Poor Spaniards," their petitions, and the erosion of privilege in late colonial Quito. *Hispanic American Historical Review* 85:595–626.

Mitchell, Don. 1997. The annihilation of space by law: The roots and implications of anti-homeless laws in the United States. *Antipode* 29:303–335.

———. 2003. *The right to the city: Social justice and the fight for public space.* New York: Guilford.

Mufune, Pempelani. 2000. Street youth in southern Africa. *International Social Science Journal* 52:233–243.

Muratorio, Blanca. 1998. Indigenous women's identities and the politics of cultural reproduction in the Ecuadorian Amazon. *American Anthropologist* 100:409–420.

Murdoch, Lydia. 2003. Begging "impostors," street theater, and the shadow economy of the Victorian city. Unpublished paper presented at the North American Victorian Studies Association (NAVSA) conference, Bloomington, Ind.

Newman, Kathe, and Elvin Wyly. 2006. The right to stay put, revisited: Gentrification and resistance to displacement in New York City. *Urban Studies* 43:23–57.

Nieuwenhuys, Olga. 1994. *Children's lifeworlds: Gender, welfare, and labor in the developing world*. New York: Routledge.

Oakley, Ann. 1994. Women and children first and last: Parallels and differences between children's and women's studies. In *Children's childhoods observed and experienced*, ed. B. Mayall, 13–32. Washington, D.C.: Falmer.

Onta-Bhatta, Lazima. 1997. Political economy, culture and violence: Children's journeys to the urban streets. *Studies in Nepali History and Society* 2:207–253.

Orlove, Benjamin S. 1998. Down to earth: Race and substance in the Andes. *Bulletin of Latin American Research* 17:207–222.

Panter-Brick, Catherine. 2002. Street children, human rights, and public health: A critique and future directions. *Annual Review of Anthropology* 31:147–171.

Peñaherrera de Costales, Piedad, Alfredo Costales Samaniego, and Fausto Jordán Bucheli. 1961. *Tungurahua*. Llacta 13. Quito: Instituto Ecuatoriano de Antropología y Geografía.

Pequeño, Andrea. 2004. Historias de misses, historias de naciones. *Íconos* 20:114–117.

Pitkin, Kathryn, and Ritha Bedoya. 1997. Women's multiple roles in economic crisis: Constraints and adaptation. *Latin American Perspectives* 24:34–49.

Platt, Tristan. 1992. Writing, shamanism and identity or voices from Abya-Yala. *History Workshop Journal*. 34:132–147.

Poeschel-Renz, Ursula. 2003. La niñez indígena frente a la desigualdad social y presión cultural. Unpublished document prepared for the Observatorio Social de Ecuador, Quito.

Ponce Jarrín, Juan. 2007. *II Informe Nacional de los Objetivos de Desarrollo del Milenio: Ecuador, Alianzas para el Desarrollo*. Quito: Centro de Investigaciones Sociales del Milenio / Programa de las Naciones Unidas para el Desarrollo / Facultad Latinoamericana de Ciencias Sociales / Secretaría Nacional de Planificación y Desarrollo.

Powers, Karen Vieira. 1995. *Andean journeys: Migration, ethnogenesis, and the state in colonial Quito*. Albuquerque: Univ. of New Mexico Press.

Pribilsky, Jason. 2001. Nervios and "modern childhood": Migration and shifting contexts of child life in the Ecuadorian Andes. *Childhood* 8:251–273.

———. 2007. *La chulla vida: Gender, migration and the family in Andean Ecuador and New York City*. Syracuse, N.Y.: Syracuse Univ. Press.

Prout, Alan, and Allison James. 1997. A new paradigm for the sociology of childhood? Provenance, promise and problems. In James and Prout 1997, 7–33.

Punch, Samantha. 2003. Youth transitions and interdependent adult-child relations in rural Bolivia. *Journal of Rural Studies* 18:123–133.

Radcliffe, Sarah. 1999. Embodying national identities: Mestizo men and white women in Ecuadorian racial-national imaginaries. *Transactions of the Institute of British Geographers* 24:213–225.

———. 2000. Entangling resistance, ethnicity, gender and nation in Ecuador. In *Entanglements of power: Geographies of domination/resistance*, ed. J. P. Sharp, P. Routledge, C. Philo, and R. Paddison, 164–181. New York: Routledge.

Radcliffe, Sarah, and Sallie Westwood. 1996. *Remaking the nation: Place, identity and politics in Latin America.* London: Routledge.

Rahier, Jean Muteba. 1998. Blackness, the racial/spatial order, migrations, and Miss Ecuador, 1995–96. *American Anthropologist* 100:421–430.

Rendón, Bolívar. 1994. *Estudio de ingresos en 10 comunidades de las Parroquias: Pasa, San Fernando, Quisapincha.* Ambato, Ecuador: CESA.

Robson, Elsbeth. 1996. Working girls and boys: Children's contributions to household survival in west Africa. *Geography* 81:403–407.

Roitman, Karem. 2004. Mestizo identity construction. Unpublished paper delivered at the meeting of the Latin American Studies Association, Las Vegas, Nev., October 7–9.

Rosaldo, Renato. 1989. Imperialist nostalgia. In *Culture and truth: The remaking of social analysis*, 68–87. Boston: Beacon.

Rose, Lionel. 1988. *"Rogues and vagabonds": Vagrant underworld in Britain, 1815–1985.* New York: Routledge.

Ruddick, Susan. 1996a. Constructing difference in public spaces: Race, class, and gender as interlocking systems. *Urban Geography* 17:132–151.

———. 1996b. *Young and homeless in Hollywood: Mapping social identities.* New York: Routledge.

Ruddick, Sue. 2003. The politics of aging: Globalization and the restructuring of youth and childhood. *Antipode* 35:334–362.

Rurevo, Rumbidzai, and Michael Bourdillon. 2003. Girls: The less visible street children of Zimbabwe. *Children, Youth and Environments* 13, no 1. http://colorado.edu/journals/cye (accessed October 25, 2003).

Sánchez-Parga, José. 2002. *Crisis en torno al Quilotoa: Mujer, cultura y comunidad.* Quito: Centro Andino de Acción Popular.

Schak, David C. 1988. *A Chinese beggars' den: Poverty and mobility in an underclass community.* Pittsburgh: Univ. of Pittsburgh Press.

Scheper-Hughes, Nancy. 1992. *Death without weeping: The violence of everyday life in Brazil.* Berkeley: Univ. of California Press.

Scheper-Hughes, Nancy, and Daniel Hoffman. 1998. Brazilian apartheid: Street kids and the struggle for urban space. In *Small wars: The cultural politics of childhood*, ed. N. Scheper-Hughes and C. Sargent, 352–388. Berkeley: Univ. of California Press.

Scheper-Hughes, Nancy, and Carolyn Sargent. 1998. Introduction: The cultural politics of childhood. In *Small wars: The cultural politics of childhood*, ed. N. Scheper-Hughes and C. Sargent, 1–33. Berkeley: Univ. of California Press.

Sibley, David. 1995. *Geographies of exclusion: Society and difference in the West.* New York: Routledge.

SIISE (Sistema Integrado de Indicadores Sociales del Ecuador). 2003a. *Analfabetismo.* Encuestas de condiciones de vida. INEC, 1999. Quito: SIISE.

———. 2003b. *Auto identificación étnico racial.* Censos de población y vivienda. INEC, 2001. Quito: SIISE.

———. 2003c. *La década de los 90s en cifras: El crecimiento económico.* BCE Cuentas nacionales, 1990–1999. Quito: SIISE.

———. 2003d. *Días que trabajan los niños/as a la semana.* Encuestas urbanas de empleo y desempleo. INEC, 2001. Quito: SIISE.

———. 2003e. *Edad de inicio del trabajo infanto-juvenil.* Encuestas urbana de empleo y desempleo. INEC, 2001. Quito: SIISE.

———. 2003f. *Empleo: Trabajo infantil y adolescente.* Encuestas de condiciones de vida: Niños de 10 a 17 Años. INEC, 1999. Quito: SIISE.

———. 2003g. *Escolaridad.* Encuestas de condiciones de vida. INEC, 1999. Quito: SIISE.

———. 2003h. *Identidad étnico-racial de los niños/as.* Mi opinión sí cuenta. DNI, 1994. Quito: SIISE.

———. 2003i. *Inflación.* Cuentas nacionales: Información estadística mensual. BCE, 1965–2001. Quito: SIISE.

———. 2003j. *Niños/as en la indigencia.* Encuestas de condiciones de vida. INEC, 1995, 1999. Quito: SIISE.

———. 2003k. *Niños/as en la pobreza.* Encuestas de condiciones de vida. INEC, 1995, 1999. Quito: SIISE.

———. 2003l. *Niños/as que aportan al ingreso del hogar.* Dirección nacional de la juventud, 1995. Quito: SIISE.

———. 2003m. *Niños/as que trabajan en la calle.* Mi opinión sí cuenta. DNI, 1994. Quito: SIISE.

———. 2003n. *Niños/as que trabajan para ayudar al ingreso familiar.* Encuestas urbanas de empleo y desempleo. INEC, 2001. Quito: SIISE.

———. 2003o. *Niños/as que trabajan y no estudian.* Encuestas de condiciones de vida. INEC, 1999. Quito: SIISE.

———. 2003p. *Repetición escolar secundaria.* Encuestas de condiciones de vida. INEC, 1995–1999. Quito: SIISE.

Silvey, Rachel. 2004. Power, difference and mobility: Feminist advances in migration studies. *Progress in Human Geography* 28:490–506.

Silvey, Rachel, and Victoria Lawson. 1999. Placing the migrant. *Annals of the Association of American Geographers* 89:121–132.

Slater, Tom. 2004. North American gentrification? Revanchist and emancipatory perspectives explored. *Environment and Planning A* 36:1191–1213.

———. 2006. The eviction of critical perspectives from gentrification research. *International Journal of Urban and Regional Research* 30:737–757.

Smith, Neil. 1996. *The new urban frontier: Gentrification and the revanchist city.* New York: Routledge.

———. 1998. Giuliani time: The revanchist 1990s. *Social Text* 57:1–20.

———. 2001. Global social cleansing: Postliberal revanchism and the export of zero tolerance. *Social Justice* 28:68–74.

———. 2002. New globalism, new urbanism: Gentrification as global urban strategy. *Antipode* 34:428–450.

Snow, David A., and Leon Anderson. 1993. *Down on their luck: A study of homeless street people*. Berkeley: Univ. of California Press.

Stedman Jones, Gareth. 1971. *Outcast London: A study in the relationship between classes in Victorian London*. Oxford: Clarendon.

Stephens, Sharon. 1995. Children and the politics of culture in "late capitalism." In *Children and the politics of culture*, ed. S. Stephens, 3–48. Princeton, N.J.: Princeton Univ. Press.

Stutzman, Ronald. 1981. El mestizaje: An all-inclusive ideology of exclusion. In *Cultural transformations and ethnicity in modern Ecuador*, ed. N. Whitten Jr., 45–94. Urbana: Univ. of Illinois Press.

Survival. 2004. Guarani suicides. CIMI-Mato Grosso do Sul. http://www.survival-international.org/guarani_suicides.htm (accessed January 2, 2005).

Swanson, Kate. 2008. Witches, children and Kiva-the-research-dog: Striking problems encountered in the field. *Area* 40:55–64.

Swanson, Katherine. 2005. Begging for dollars in Gringopampa: Geographies of gender, race, ethnicity and childhood in the Ecuadorian Andes. PhD diss., Univ. of Toronto, Dept. of Geography.

Taylor, Monique. 2002. *Harlem: Between heaven and hell*. Minneapolis: Univ. of Minnesota Press.

Terrio, Susan. 2004. Migration, displacement, and violence: Prosecuting Romanian street children at the Paris Palace of Justice. *International Migration* 42:5–33.

Tester, Frank James, and Paule McNicoll. 2004. Isumagijaksaq: Mindful of the state; Social constructions of Inuit suicide. *Social Science & Medicine* 58:2625–2636.

Tibán, Lourdes. 2001. Dimensión cultural y derechos de la niñez y de la adolescencia indígena. In *Memorias*, ed. Berenice Cordero, 63–64. Encuentro Subregional por la Niñez y la Adolescencia Indígena, July 12–13. Quito: UNICEF / Fundación Rigoberta Menchú / FLASCO-Ecuador.

Tibanlombo, Juan. 1996. San Gonzalo: La brujería y la muerte. *Diario Hoy* (Quito), July 18, 2A.

Tomic, Patricia, Ricardo Trumper, and Rodrigo Hidalgo Dattwyler. 2006. Manufacturing modernity: Cleaning, dirt, and neoliberalism in Chile. *Antipode* 38:508–529.

Uitermark, Justus, and Jan Willem Duyvendak. 2008. Civilising the city: Populism and revanchist urbanism in Rotterdam. *Urban Studies* 45:1485–1503.

UNICEF. 2004. Childhood defined: Childhood under threat; The state of the world's children 2005. http://www.unicef.org/sowc05/english/childhooddefined.html (accessed December 10, 2004).

El Universo. 2002. Jaime Nebot: Guayaquil es un ejemplo para el país. June 30. http://www.eluniverso.com (accessed March 25, 2005).

———. 2003. Cámaras vigilan el ordenamiento. September 25. http://www.eluniverso.com. (accessed March 25, 2005).

———. 2004a. Disputa entre alcalde, empresarios y policía en Guayaquil: La seguridad en crisis. Guayaquil. November 26. http://www.eluniverso.com (accessed March 25 2005).

———. 2004b. William Bratton: Se necesita mejorar calidad de policías. March 2. http://www.eluniverso.com (accessed March 25, 2005).

Uzendoski, Michael. 2005. *The Napo Runa of Amazonian Ecuador*. Urbana: Univ. of Illinois Press.

Valentine, Gill. 1996. Children should be seen and not heard: The production and transgression of adults' public space. *Urban Geography* 17:205–220.

Van Vleet, Krista E. 2003. Adolescent ambiguities and the negotiation of belonging in the Andes. *Ethnology* 42:349–363.

Vásconez, Alison, and Fabricio Proaño. 2002. *Trabajo infantil y juvenil: Diagnóstico de la problemática de niños y adolescentes de 6 a 18 años en situación de riesgo y de los programas existentes*. Quito: Facultad Latino Americana de Ciencias Sociales, Sede Ecuador.

Wacquant, Loic. 2003. Towards a dictatorship over the poor? Notes on the penalization of poverty in Brazil. *Punishment & Society* 5:197–205.

Wade, Peter. 2002. *Race, nature and culture: An anthropological perspective*. Sterling, England: Pluto.

Wardhaugh, Julia. 1996. "Homeless in Chinatown": Deviance and social control in Cardboard City. *Sociology* 30:701–716.

Weismantel, Mary. 1988. *Food, gender and poverty in the Ecuadorian Andes*. Philadelphia: Univ. of Pennsylvania Press.

———. 1995. Making kin: Kinship theory and Zumbagua adoptions. *American Ethnologist* 22:685–704.

———. 2001. *Cholas and Pishtacos: Stories of race and sex in the Andes*. Chicago: Univ. of Chicago Press.

Weiss, Wendy. 1997. Debt and devaluation: The burden on Ecuador's popular class. *Latin American Perspectives*. 24:9–33.

Whiteford, Linda M. 1998. Children's health as accumulated capital: Structural adjustment in the Dominican Republic and Cuba. In *Small wars: The cultural politics of childhood*, ed. N. Scheper-Hughes and C. Sargent, 186–201. Berkeley: Univ. of California Press.

Whitten, Norman E. Jr. 2003. Introduction. In *Millennial Ecuador: Critical essays on cultural transformations and social dynamics*, ed. N. Whitten Jr., 1–45. Iowa City: Univ. of Iowa Press.

Wibbelsman, Michelle. 2003. Appendix: General information on Ecuador. In *Millennial Ecuador: Critical essays on cultural transformations and social dynamics*, ed. N. Whitten Jr., 375–387. Iowa City: Univ. of Iowa Press.

Willis, Katie, and Brenda Yeoh. 2000. *Gender and migration*. Cheltenham, England: Elgar.

Wilson, Fiona. 2004. Indian citizenship and the discourse of hygiene/disease in nineteenth-century Peru. *Bulletin of Latin American Research* 23:165–180.

Wilson, David, and Dennis Grammenos. 2005. Gentrification, discourse, and the body: Chicago's Humboldt Park. *Environment and Planning D: Society and Space* 23:295–312.

Wilson, James, and George Kelling. 1982. Broken windows. *Atlantic Monthly*, March, 1–10.

Wogan, Peter. 2004. *Magical Writing in Salasaca: Literacy and Power in Highland Ecuador*. Boulder: Westview.

Wyly, Elvin, and Daniel Hammel. 2004. Gentrification, segregation, and discrimination in the American urban system. *Environment and Planning A* 36:1215–1241.

Yeoh, Brenda S. A., and Shirlena Huang. 1998. Negotiating public space: Strategies and styles of migrant female domestic workers in Singapore. *Urban Studies* 35:583–602.

Zamosc, Leon. 1994. Agrarian protest and the Indian movement in the Ecuadorian highlands. *Latin American Research Review* 29:37–66.

INDEX

Note: Illustrations are indicated by an *f* after the page number; tables similarly are indicated by *t*.

LaVergne, TN USA
08 March 2010

175124LV00004BA/13/P